# LATE
# MARRIAGE
# PRESS

# .PILFER.

*a memoir*

Pablo D'Stair

LATE
MARRIAGE
PRESS

Copyright © 2021 Pablo D'Stair

All rights reserved. No part of this book may be reproduced, stored in a retrieval system or transmitted in any form or by any means without the prior written permission of the publishers, except by a reviewer who may quote brief passages in a review to be printed in newspaper, magazine or journal.

First Edition
ISBN: 979-8-3484-4482-2

Published by Late Marriage Press

for Remy, Constantine, Hugo, Hermann, Roquentin,
Carlyle, Giles, Paul, Vincente, Winston, Lucio,
and both Pablos

**AUTHOR'S NOTE**

The decision to call all parties mentioned in this volume, including myself, by invented names is purely aesthetic. For context on one scene, I explain here how, at the time of the depicted events, my name was Pablo Gonzalez-Fernandez. Every word in this volume is true.

.PILFER.

Damn that Void
It's right on me
That goddamned Void
That hanging tree

**GOODLOE BYRON**

.part one.

.1.

I STOLE TWENTY DOLLARS FROM my mom's purse. A single, crisp bill. I was five years old.

My mom was out front of the house, talking with the parents of one of my friends. It was the dull of evening. The cul-du-sac where we lived was serene. If I had to animate it, it'd be in hues of green evoking near twilight.

I recall the light from the chandelier hung above the dining table. For the thirty-five years since the crime, I've thought of the color of that light. Brown-orange. Orange-brown. White soured beige and burnt. I fell in love with the color of that light, I think. A deep love.

It was that light which made me want to be a painter.

Something I never became.

The only witness to the crime was my infant brother. He was laid witless in a carrier, there on the dining room table.

When I think of the time, I see him as awake.

But who can say?

I suppose the mind bends toward narrative, drama.

Regard: thoughtless and looking up at the chandelier light, my infant brother, awake.

The purse, I think, was green. But I don't recall, so will not say so. Green stands out to me. But so does leather. Leather stands out, though only for me to remark how I think to myself 'No, I don't think it was leather.'

Countless times these thirty-five years I've thought that.

Then I'll think 'It certainly wasn't cloth, wasn't knit'.

I recall zippers, but also believe there were none. A snap-button. Classic brass. Classic something-like-brass.

But I may've been thinking, all these years, of a slick, winter vest my mom often wore. That was green. A winter vest with cold snap-buttons. Maybe brass. Something-like.

I didn't have to open the purse. The money was there in a wallet tucked in a wide, sloping pouch. More than one bill, so I figured the crime would be perfect. Not everything gone. Just something gone. One part of something.

Who would suspect me?

Who would even notice?

How would they not doubt themselves?

Their minds would invent a scenario which made sense. Oblige them to shoulder the blame.

Careless of them. Be more cautious, in future.

Here was the birth, the evolution of a *regret*.

My older brother was someplace, so the filching needed to be swift. Fingers to money. Money to closed fist. Me up the staircase to the bedroom.

But was it?

Upstairs?

The bedroom, then?

When I recall secreting the bill inside my pillowcase, I recall the bedroom being upstairs. Years and years make me doubt the accuracy of this, though.

Was it upstairs, my tucking the money, arm slipped up to elbow around pillow under pillowcase?

Upstairs my rearranging the position of everything to seem innocent?

Upstairs my certainty the pillowcase would be the first place anyone would look?

Upstairs where *anyplace* seemed the first place anyone would look?

Under the mattress.

Inside a sock.

The sensations of those moments had the wet weight to them of a coming bowel movement.

Then back downstairs and outside.

Distancing myself from the act.

I recall the sky, which I might this time animate blue. Animate to suggest droplets of ink spreading to discolor milk left standing in a small orange cup.

The crime was already discovered by the time I re-entered the house from where I'd loitered by the pricker-bushes. By the pricker-bushes, under the power-lines.

In such spot, during the day, behind me, would've been the constant sizzle of honeybee threat. From a larger bush beside the house at the row-end the wall of which we'd often throw balls against.

But it was evening.

Dusked silence.

Scent of charcoal from someplace. Me watching the wink of airplanes making pace in directions away.

On walking back toward the house it'd struck me I ought to've hidden the money outside. How if it wasn't found in the pillowcase, people would suspect I'd hid it in the bushes or buried it under the soil. But it would take awhile for them to suspect this. By then I could've hidden it elsewhere.

Why would my mom have looked in her purse, right then?

Why count her money?

We'd only just returned home from being out on errands. There was nothing to purchase in our dining room. It should've been next morning, afternoon, by the time money even occurred to her. She should've been someplace else when the discrepancy was noted. A timeline free of me should've elapsed between my deed and her confusion over her count.

The senselessness of her action baffled me.

Here was a world turned betrayal. The very air an inherent snitch.

Had I seen the money? I was asked.

What money and why would I have?

To prove it, I helped look. Dutifully went to hands-and-knees on hardwood floor as though scoffing. As though about to pick up the so-called missing money from the obvious place it'd carelessly fallen.

Had my older brother seen the money? he was asked when he ambled around to the crime-scene.

He had not.

I could've hissed from how I could tell he was instantly believed.

Why?

Why believe him?

I'd never thought to pin the theft on my brother nor to use his existence to spread uncertainty over my being the culprit. Not until that moment, anyway.

In that moment those possibilities dawned on me.

But at the time of the theft, no.

The theft had been blood-borne.

Yet still: to know, sense, to understand my brother was above suspicion as much as I was clearly under it riled me.

If I could steal, he could steal.

If he hadn't, who else was there to suspect but me?

If I hadn't, should it not follow, who else was there to suspect but him?

He turned out his pockets without being asked.

I followed suit.
Well, the money was someplace.
My mom was looking and looking.
No doubt wondering why I'd walked to the pricker-bushes.
No doubt already scheming to get the truth out of me.
She must've been. The things to think were obvious. It was only a matter of time until they were thought.
My fate was an utter inevitability. Even then, freshly criminal, five years old, I understood this.
And felt I had been wronged.

I HADN'T STOLEN THE MONEY for the money of it. Or better say, that's precisely why I had. Better yet: I'd stolen it for the *it* of it.

I'd merely wanted artifact. Succulent paper to be mine. My fingers in trace along the fibers' powdery stiff fronts and backs. Scent from the bill, luscious as gasoline or the remnant of pencil erasure, stinging my nostrils whenever I'd please.

I'd wanted the money the same as I might want to keep a lost tooth, even someone else's. The same as I wished I could have a doorknob not attached to any door. Something I'd no way of reasonably asking for, even as a birthday gift.

A doorknob? How absurd. What for?
I did consider returning the money.
That night I mulled the possibility over and over.
By the following night it was pointless to entertain the notion.
Certainly I couldn't be the one to've suddenly found it some obscure place. Likewise, it served to reason how if anyone else found it their immediate thought upon its discovery would be 'How unnatural it is this would be here'.

No matter the clever location I came up with for the bill to be stumbled upon, it must've been put there to be found. No other conclusion. This being so, it must've been put there by me.

The Suspect.

I'd be confronted, all the same.

No point admitting the truth under such conditions.

Alternately?

I'd maybe not be approached. The matter would go unremarked. No follow-up.

Though knowing someone knew and was doing nothing with the knowledge gave me the creeps.

Neither path would keep me the twenty, regardless.

Between confession, apology, and silence, silence was most romantic. Most honest.

I wasn't sorry, so what use forgiveness?

If not apologizing, what use confession?

I'd have to play a pretend of remorse. Or else I'd have to flagrantly insist 'Well, I shouldn't be' when told I was absolved.

I was returning the object, not regretting my taking it.

I was regretting returning it, in fact.

I'd need to explain that in order to be honest.

Then?

I'd hear I was forgiven anyway. Forgiven for not apologizing. Praised for doing the good thing.

Or maybe I'd be punished further.

Or both.

Not that punishment mattered to me, if I'm being truthful. That I recall with absolute clarity. There were no fears of consequence.

What could consequence be?

I'd already have lost what I'd wanted. Only myself to blame. I'd controlled *take*. I'd controlled *return*.

What else was there?

Some punitive measure in addition to not having the bill?

Anything like that would fall into the randomness of life, no connection to the act under discussion.

Sure, I'll not play outside.

Videogames aren't available to me this week, okay.
I'd be disallowed whatever someone told me I'd be disallowed.
I could just as well look at the world as though those things, whatever they were, had never been options to begin with.
What difference?
I wasn't even genuinely anxious by middle next day.
It was a game, soon enough.
Keep the money hid until I could disappear it entire.
Spend it.
Not because that's why I'd swiped it. Just because that was expected. The only sensible way to make the theft mean anything.
Mean anything to anyone else.
Casting the paper away, tearing it up would be a loss.
Absurd.
To me, to everyone.
Now that I was down this path, I liked having, liked keeping the twenty. The desire to do so was more powerful than the desire to obtain it had been.
But I couldn't keep it.
My possessing it and the joy found in such possession was transient.
So I had to repurpose the situation, rejigger the joy.
Were I caught after spending it, I could entertain myself going along with my apprehender's belief that they knew why I'd done it. What I'd wanted. What I wanted. Relish their incorrectness in thinking I was born typical.
What did I do?
Learned all the ways a five-year-old can't spend twenty dollars for trying.
It's silly, perfectly silly in the glorious way only theft is.
I might roam, for example, the Drugstore, older brother along or just me with mom or with dad. Might do my best to hustle myself some moment of privacy. Lace along down this aisle and

that on the excuse I was popping to the water fountain. Peruse the racks of trifles. Might try to think of something to buy.

Buy?

How would I do that?

I caught sight, for example, of a box of Valentine's Day cards. Lovely and plain. Resplendently generic. I coveted the sensation of tearing the flimsy rectangles free of each other along perforations *tick-tick-tick*. Folding them. Stacking them. Opening. Closing. Stuffing my pockets with a bunch. Filling each card's face with imaginary messages or drawings meant for concocted entities of my fancy. Not even messages *From* me or *To* me. Instead pretending I'd lucked across love notes from strangers. Interceptions I could guess over, ponder, keep from being delivered, alter, forge.

No way to be guaranteed I'd have time to get to the cash register without my parents, my brother spotting me.

How about if the clerk told me I needed a parent on hand in order to buy something, per Store Policy?

Or what if this same clerk mentioned my earlier purchase when I had to return to the line, family in tow?

Nevermind how I'd have nowhere to put the bag, no way to explain having the item on me if I did pull off the transaction.

Impossible.

But this impossibility nonetheless put in my mind the possibility of having change dispensed to me.

Coins. Different, smaller bills.

Maybe I could, over time, pass these into my life, one-by-one. As though come across organically. Break singles for quarters to play arcade games with. This might hardly be noticed spread out over months.

There were machines which could translate singles into four quarters. At the Doughnut Shop, for example. Not that I had any way of getting to the Doughnut Shop on my own. But there was also the Pizzeria. When out for dinner, my dad would often give me one single to break. I could use the opportunity to break two or three of my own without raising a flag.

Or maybe for a jape I could return the money to my mom's purse. Coin-by-coin. Single-by-single. Grin idiotic at her never being the wiser she'd got back what had so vexed her to lose.

There were many things I might do.

If I broke the twenty.

Zero ways to break the twenty was the reality.

Because that action would be the most peculiar thing imaginable.

A five-year-old asking someone to make change with no risk of it being mentioned to a parent?

I'd no idea how to manipulate the world around to it.

'For my dad' I might say to a clerk or 'For my mom'.

It seemed simple. But for such conversation to transpire it'd require me to be someplace with a clerk without my parents.

Who and what I was hamstrung me from executing any plan.

I was a thief who was a child.

A mind without a body, more-or-less.

CONSIDERATIONS ABOUT WHAT THE MONEY might be spent on became more abstract. Thoughts concerning methods with which to keep the money hidden turned more concrete. The typical purpose of Twenty-Dollar Bill was no more. Even if through miraculous circumstance I could spend it, I wouldn't.

A new preoccupation sprouted.

It must be made real-and-unreal, the money.

Kept at the outskirts of existing.

Suspected spent, suspected hid.

Perpetually fluctuating in the minds of those who gave it consideration until maybe it and its theft were forgotten.

Perhaps I would eventually bury it someplace. Outside. By the pricker-bushes. Under the power-lines. Forget it myself. Not spent, destroyed. Just there. Interred. Life done. Eternal.

Yes. Clear as lark song I recall all this dawning on me.

A fascination.

I was bursting to share my mind with some cohort but couldn't. Trust wasn't feasible. Sharing would destroy equilibrium. The state, now existing, could only endure. It was my job to allow its endurance. Inviting anyone to share in what I knew would queer things. My function was to exercise restraint.

I recall so keenly how I felt myself becoming a simmer of anxious noia. Perpetual nerves over me. Not unpleasant, though. To the contrary. I recollect, even as the child I was, the squirming comfort of my life being defined by what my life was hiding. The new way I knew myself. Intrinsic as cell structure, comfortable as bathed skin.

Time took its cues from my anxieties, arranged itself around the hiding of the bill. Morning, afternoon, evening, night had each their own antsy drum-beat.

My purpose was to discover every neat little cranny where the object might be hid. This day here. That day there. Given enough days, the thing might've found its way into every crevice of the house.

Such rambunctious joy in learning all the spots of the world around me which were ancillary. So much superfluous world surrounding our lives.

How often had this cabinet been opened?

Had anyone looked at, touched the books on this shelf in my lifetime?

Was it for some purpose a long-expired bottle of cough syrup had never been tossed in the trash bin?

All the coats, no longer worn, in the main floor closet?

I'd slip the bill into their interior pockets. Secret it, folded in half and in-half-again, up their sleeves.

In this same closet, I'd slip the bill inside shoes, boots I'd never see anyone use. Wedge it under a bag of thick salt meant for winter weather which'd been there who knows for how long.

This location, the closet, more than any other, beguiled.

Taught me the most.

Because it carried some risk.

Wasn't it only a guess that these garments weren't worn?

That no one had present-day use for this crusted hard potting soil?

That a jug of candy-blue antifreeze wouldn't be hefted up exactly the day I chose it for the bill's security?

Or how would it go were I observed fiddling about in there?

Noticed offhand more than once?

My presence anyplace would clue anyone else there was something to look into. Me someplace I seemed odd could only mean one thing, after all.

The closet was a touchpoint with contemporary purpose while at once being a mausoleum. Taught me how so was the world. Illustrated how everything gathered dust in its way. This dust was coat-shaped. That dust was a dropped soda can no one bothered to set back to the trash-bag. Some other was a snip of shoelace cut when it couldn't be unknotted.

Time itself gathered dust.

Past and Present.

The promise that the Present would be the Past once the Future took over.

Past would retain Present's features.

Every inch of Time individual.

Stacking. Nothing changing. Just new buds of existence from previous existence. Multiplicative.

Time was Time's own dust.

I would also explore the closets in my parents' bedroom.

One was my mom's, exclusively. The one which seemed never

open unless it was me folding its accordion doors. The one which had a smell of disuse, interior. Everything preserved. Antiseptic. Like formalin-filled specimen jars hung the cramped dresses, trousers, sweaters covered in plastic wrappings. A top shelf had boxes stacked in which there were old hats, photographs.

Old hats. Photographs. A shy twenty-dollar bill.

The same bashful twenty which taught me the thickness of the lace sleeves of the gown my mom had worn to her wedding as I tucked it inside one.

In-and-out of history forgotten or else history stored for safe keeping or else history stored for safe keeping and forgotten the stolen bill slipped.

The money snuggled also into my dad's socks-and-underthings drawer. It went into tissue boxes, delicately pinned underneath soft squares awaiting nose-blow. Went into an old wicker sewing basket the contents of which were thought of as indecipherable curio by my older brother and I who had never known a button sewn between us. Even as I hid the bill and smiled, thumbing the spools of colored thread, the scissors, the circular cutters, the items were curiosities which stoked no true curiosity.

Places and things were just places and things lost to purpose.

Except to be places to stash other things.

Within the laundry room I discovered the most ancillary, purposeless place of all. Not the room itself, no. The laundry room had its clear purpose. Or a fleck of it did. The washer, dryer, a deep gulleted sink, and two sodden shelves all barely shown by a lethargic bulb which buzzed its phlegmy brown.

The light which showed the machines, sink, the shelving hardly bothered to dress visible. It seemed present enough only to make the shadows around it over-pronounced, cockney. The scent surrounding the washer seemed to've drifted from the dark environment skirting it. A fragrance which befit the chill of protoplasm.

The portion of the room cordoned off by the shadows was easy to think of as its own separate building. This area seemed ponderously large, long. My memory of it is impossible to physics except those of a child in the pitch hiding money.

Easy also to think of the space as haunted. Crawling with life that needed nothing but itself to survive. Metal storage racks with file-folders, trinkets, luggage-cases, and evidences of insects along them. Bunched in, tight. One atop the other.

Every time I left the place, I felt myself itching with things imagined which also were not.

At the lip of the laundry room, I found my boldest hiding spot, one I nearly made myself sick over by waiting an entire day before checking back on. A day waited through like any other except it was twelve-thousand miles long.

There was a crank-operated pencil sharpener mounted to the doorframe. A holy thing to me. A favorite Icon. The casing meant to collect the talcum soft shavings was long gone. On the floor, in a pile the consistency of fresh anthills, stood a ponderous mound of pencil powder.

Sometimes my older brother and I giddily ground pencils down for the sheer pleasure of watching the unblinking mechanism of the serrated grinders twirl like a choking barber pole. Pencil-after-pencil devoured. Normal pencils. Colored ones. Their essence snowing floorward. For a laugh sometimes we might even try a pen, a marker, a birthday candle, a straw, the arm of an action figure.

Delicately I shifted the pile of soot to one side. Patted the twenty to the cold slate floor. Shifted the mound back to bury the bill. Tinkered, fretted with the look of the pile. Tried to make it resemble an arrangement from nature instead of one willed by my hand.

I ground down more pencils. More pencils more pencils.

Finally had to leave it to chance.

Such delectable gnashing. One night of headache sleeplessness and stomach in gunfire of nausea. One night which I remember as a saga.

Hadn't I better go down there before morning?

Before school?

So many things might go wrong.

But also I wanted to be caught this way, if any.

Such absurdity would be the most perfect in which to be apprehended.

I'd loved this night while I'd endured it. Adored it the way I did the dreams from a fever. Those special concoctions thrown up by my mind which I thanked my ailing body for causing. Those dreams which made me wish nothing but illness for myself when they filled me.

That night it was as though I was awake for a dream.

Was awake for a dream from which I wished to never awaken.

OF COURSE TIME, AS EVER it was, is cagey. Never moreso than in remembering five-year-old days thirty-five years on.

Was all that weeks?

It surely couldn't have been a month.

Month-and-change?

Preposterous I would've carried on with a stolen twenty-dollar bill so long as that.

It couldn't have been days, merely. Days in youth were always so individuated. Each its own episode. All of them furlongs wide. As a kid I know my mind was able to mix any one to any other no better than green crayon wax would blend with orange.

Yet now?

Thinking back now?

They're of a unit, those days. Childhood itself a single image made of scribbled scrawl in every color. If I stare, I can individuate pigments. But Lord help me to know which squaggle is above, beneath another.

It amuses me to think I might've built a month's worth of memory out of some few days. Hidden the loot multiple places over the course of a solitary twenty-four hours, twelve, eight. Lost in a Swedenborgian Space. Might've roamed the house, sniffing out spot and spot and spot, but only stashed the bill in a handful of them.

It's so immediate how the moment forms in my mind of the end of it. Yes, this moment is distinct. Individual. Can be summoned pristine. But nothing at all from a time just prior or a time immediately afterward.

Blink.

It was there. I was there. Almost irrelevant I'd ever been elsewhere.

Blink.

I found myself sat with my older brother beside me. Our mom just upstairs, bathing.

Blink.

The beginning of my physical existence, I think.

Was it that I was waiting my turn for the bath?

This is how I've always recalled it. These thirty-five years. It makes sense, anyway. Other memories of sitting on the stairs in wait for my turn in the tub are enough to make me certain it was so this day. No matter if the event as I recall it is telescoped, condensed, quilted from many memories. Those other times waiting for bathwater serve well enough to conjure themselves as reasonable prologue to this incident.

My recollection is of middle late-afternoon. But only because I know the memory of waiting on the stairs for my bath another specific time was at night. Those memories colored different than each other. That night most of the lights in the house had been doused. That time, not this time. This time I sat chatting in remembered brightness. The same linen crisp illumination captured in a beloved photograph of my brother and I on these stairs.

Our conversation was idle. Whatever almost nine-year-olds and five-year-olds find to gab about.

However it was, whatever we spoke about, what it came to was my brother scootched close for sibling intimacy, his voice lowered to suggest his concern for my security.

He asked me hadn't I taken the twenty dollars from our mom's purse. He knew I had, he explained. Simply because he knew he hadn't.

This served to reason. Logic and reality pincered me.

It was absurd to mount a straight denial, here.

To say nothing seemed equally outlandish.

Without a third point-of-reference involved, an accusation from the outside rather than a query from the one other possible culprit who knew well his own innocence, there was no game, no purpose.

To lie here didn't compute.

My older brother's face was the warmth of an oven preheated and left standing. 'It must be a burden' he sighed, features gummy with camaraderie. He entreated me to allow him in on the secret so it might be jointly contended.

All at once a strum of emotions quavered in me, violin string tight.

I should tell him I'd swiped the bill. We could be partners. Of course he was correct. A burden. Too much to keep suppressed inside myself. A burial with no terminus, not dirt enough to ever be finished the grave.

Why cloister myself to a lonely otherworld it was preposterous to dwell in forever?

I did want to share with someone. The only sensible next step was to bring someone else in, pass the money to them. Maybe this was best. He could use the money. It would be easy to break the bill were the two of us involved.

That he, my brother, had come to me was quite moving. The

feeling wasn't joy like I'd experienced in the days or weeks or months I'd been alone, but instead an emotion without name or feature I feel swell in me every time I think back to this moment.

'Yes' I told him. Very simply. Quietly. 'I took the money.'

I would share it with him. Give it to him. Gladly.

My brother stood.

I recall him rising. The snap of it. The sensation of the sight of him getting to his feet was like I'd suddenly shrunk. An old Claymation special effect.

'Mom!' my brother bellowed 'Jasper stole the money!'

He didn't look down at me. Back at me. His motion was jack-in-the-box. Fluid. Four five six steps up to knock on the bathroom door. Calling out through it again how I was the thief.

I'm certain I cried returning the bill, though I don't recall it specifically. I don't recall the incident of forking over what I'd stolen, at all. The presence of all the other events I do recall cleanly proves it. A point in my life shown by echo-location. A sonar blip.

What I know is that any tears weren't about guilt or shame over the transgression I was caught in. Any tears were about guilt and shame over the failure I knew I was.

Guilt for abandoning myself.

Shame for not understanding until caged how not only should I have expected such an outcome, I should've caused it.

Chosen it.

Controlled it.

The moment was predestined. But it ought to've been predestined with my consent.

If I'd truly chosen to share the money, had taken that path as an option forward of my own considered accord, then my brother's betrayal wouldn't have been a betrayal. Only a continuation of my act. Had I shared the theft with him on my own steam, I could've allowed him to turn me in or for us to find cahoots. Had

I been thinking clearly, I should've been always in wait of his making this gambit to join me or to backstab.

I'd gotten lost in my hide-and-seek. So enamored of myself I'd forgotten there was more than myself. There was a world which saw me but didn't know me. A world I existed in and didn't. I'd lost track how there were people I needed to know didn't know me beyond how I entertained.

That night I stewed in righteous indignation over my idiocy. Gnashed my teeth, hurling whispered abuses at myself into my breath dampened pillowcase.

There had been so many other paths forward I'd overlooked, just flat ignored.

How had I stopped, satisfied to simply hide hide hide hide hide?

I should've known my brother was up to something just for it being possible he might've been.

So why hadn't I slipped the bill into his pant pocket, he none the wiser?

When they were already in the laundry, for example. My mom would've found the bill. Then I'd have seen how things played out. Have arranged the prestige, the denouement.

Better still, I ought to've gotten it into his jacket pocket one day before he left for school. He would've found it on himself. I could've waited to see his choice. His *honest* choice. Seen how my choice made him choose.

I should never have stopped at concealing my act but instead have forced it into the life of those who asked for it by poking their noses about as though different than me.

That galled me.

Knowing there were those who thought they were different than me but who didn't understand a thing.

No.

Everyone. They weren't different than me.

I was different than them.

.2.

WE LEARNED ABOUT UNITS. The composition of numbers. Of things. In school. Kindergarten. Again in first-grade.

*One* wasn't really *One*.

The teacher handed out wooden squares resembling waffles which represented this.

This waffle was *One* as the one-hundred fused bits of itself.

Then there were sticks of ten bits. Aptly called *tenths*. Ten of those sticks made the one *One*.

We'd stack ten of these *tenths* on top of the one *One* to facilitate full comprehension.

I'd hold the waffle block. Pretend to be snapping off a *tenth* as though it were a sugar-wafer coated in chocolate. I'd then hold a tenth-stick, wanting to ingest it, my saliva furious when I couldn't even give the thing a nibble.

Most beautiful were single-unit wood blocks. Cubes the size of my childhood thumbnail.

These were named *hundredths*.

Or when they were part of a tenth-stick were named *tenths*.

That is, when the tenth-stick meant *One*, proper, the hundredth-block meant *Ten*.

They were sublime, the singles.

Breathtaking.

A perfect, generic color of *wood*. The inviolate, ordinary shape and stiffness of *cube*. In their every featureless respect they were miracles.

Despite following why they were called this time *hundredths* that time *tenths,* I called them, all the time, *oneths*.

The teacher thought I didn't understand what was being discussed.

She split the difference with me, eventually. I was right insofar as they represented the *ones-place* of a number.

A truth, I'd no doubt.

An irrelevant one.

I didn't care about math.

Math was meant to represent the world.

These cubes were fugitives from someplace beyond it.

I could hardly think of a more sacrosanct thing than these miniscule wooden blocks. There was a jug of them I'd have killed to've forced my hand down into. Dig around to the wrist, the forearm. Like an insect scooping through a teensy bucket of sand grains.

I wanted to stuff my pockets bloat with these *oneths*.

Fill a pillowcase with them. Squeeze my fingers to it. Hug my arms around. Use it to rest my head upon at night.

Or I'd pour the pillowcase out, stand barefoot in the spill whenever I'd please. Dump it on myself, laid in an empty bathtub. Squirm. My back grinding to wood grinding to porcelain tub base.

I'd dribble handfuls of *oneths* on me like water droplets wrung from a washcloth.

We were not given one-hundred of the single-units to lay overtop of the waffled *One*. Only ten to arrange across the tenth-stick.

I'd tap ten *oneths* to perfect alignment along the stick.

Disturb the alignment.

Correct it.

Try to poke the third-in-line free without upsetting the arrangement of its nine friends.

I asked could I have some of the *oneths*.

Have?

To keep.

No.

Could I have one *oneth*, at least?

No.

Instead of recess outside could I stay indoors to play with the jug of them?

No.

What about during indoor recess?

Instead of puzzles, toys, could I play with them, then?

No. They weren't *toys*. They were *math supplies*.

I could help myself to the building blocks, though.

All different shapes. Colors. Sizes. An abundant variety of worthlessnesses. No thanks.

The world, again, had proved itself to be utter madness.

Stealing one *oneth* during class should've been simple. Except for devilish precautions taken seemingly to daunt exactly that.

For homework we weren't given any blocks to take. Worked out the same problems as in class but with cut squares of worksheet paper and glue stick.

In class, the teacher roamed the room. Forever glancing around. Like to be helpful. Attentive.

We students were doled out the appropriate amount of each block type for whichever exercise being proctored. Ten *hundredths*, ten *tenths*, one *One*.

Our tables sat four people. One dubbed a leader. Who made it a point to count the blocks at the end of the work session. That was where they found their pride.

Even if not for this safeguard, I couldn't keep an eye on everyone. No way of knowing was I being casually glanced.

It was too intimidating an atmosphere.
Maybe I could arrange to slip a *oneth* to my pocket.
Thought about inching one up my sleeve.
Or else keeping one palmed when returning them. Enacting a pantomime of 'Where did it go?' even if the leader was dogged, steadfast about counting.
Or I might drop one *oneth* to the floor. Set shoe-bottom firm overtop it. Could time this for right after the initial disbursement. Politely chime 'I only have nine' then be given one extra. At some moment after this ruse, I'd perform like I was itching my ankle. Slip the *oneth* under my foot inside my shoe. Bask in the sharp triumph of each step the rest of the day.
The more elaborate my method of theft, of course, the less I'd be able to explain myself if one thing went wrong.
Plus, even if I could've snuck a *oneth* into my pocket, the truth was I needed more than one. At least enough to close my fist around. Feel the tense friction of flats and corner sharps against each other.
The *oneths* ought belong to me.
I loved them.
A love far beyond any mere function they might serve educationally.
To this class they were inconsequential but guarded like gold bricks.
Even the fact that I might snatch one but could never snatch ten or twelve was an insult.
Could I swipe one-a-day?
The Math unit utilizing them only lasted a five-day week.
Four days left by the time I was starting up my planning.
Two-a-day?
Three?
Such nonsense, this being something I'd be caught at.
How could so understandable an act carry a penalty?

How could my desire be for the exact something the world conspired to make it impossible I might possess?

The blocks didn't come from anyplace I had access to.

At the Supermarket, Toy Store, there were blocks, sure, but not these scrumptiously ordinary, beige cubes.

These nothings.

These nothings which represented less-than-a-thing to the world.

Them being no place else almost made it sensible to me why they'd be so protected at school.

If they were cherished like I cherished them it would make sense.

But that wasn't why.

The reason why, like most everything else, had nothing to do with anything real or pulsing.

They just belonged to somebody.

If I had my hands on some and then one day found them missing, I'd not begrudge them being gone. Curse or hunt down whoever took them.

I'd be fine with someone stealing them. I'd understand.

If only they could be mine awhile first.

THERE WAS NO END TO the things that I wanted. Objects. Specifics. The main identifying trait of the bunch was that they couldn't be had. That there'd be no reason for them.

I wanted things which were nothing in-and-of themselves. Things for which I had no purpose except to have. Adore. Understand richly and my own.

I wanted them.

Without asking.

Without explaining myself.

Without affecting any pretense which would make my request seem conforming to why they should be wanted.

It was miniscule portions of the world I'd set my heart on. My head perpetually a cauldron of plans to steal things nobody could give me even if I asked for. Every day I spent cataloguing the treasures around me which were nothing to anyone and yet couldn't be mine.

I wanted the hands off a clock.

The less decorative the better. The most general hands from the most ordinary clock.

The hands from the clocks on the walls of the school.

Those sniffling red sticks, shivering off seconds. The brittle, uncooked spaghetti of them. They'd be like procuring rare whiskers off an imaginary cat. I wanted to have several laid in a drawer. Roll the pads of my index fingers over them. Test their delicate give by bending them between thumb and forefinger. I wanted to snap one. To snap ten. Have twenty pieces of the red whiskers of a clock.

I ached to swipe the sponges from Art class. Triangles. But not simply regular sponges cut that shape. These sponges came as triangles. *Were* triangles. I yearned for a bucketful, all stained to the mud of awkward off-rainbows from use. Could picture myself alone at home. Sat to my bed. Stacking them as though paying out a currency to someone for a job well done. Receiving them as barter for supplies.

Or else I wanted the circles being emptied from the flimsy bottom of the librarian's three-hole punch. To put in my pocket. To have. To have *holes*. To litter holes into a mud puddle. Enough to fill a cereal bowl with. Add a little milk to. Dump down the sink after chewing a soggy spoonful, spitting it out.

I wanted the ancient, bent, laminated *Bathroom Pass*. To carry it in my pocket. Ready to present at any time. I'd wield the pointless authority of the glorious object over the world. Even now my chest tightens with desire for it.

My mom would take me along to the Garden Center.

Magnificent decorations abounded.

I'd scheme to prise pieces free of the largers they were part of.

Couldn't stand it how there'd be such horrendous repercussions were I to attempt, be caught out.

The cuckoo from a clock.

What could be more exquisite to have?

Little wooden, little tin village streets lined with accents shaped like wreaths, frogs, firewood bundles, snowballs.

I wanted to pocket the phony, miniature burlap bags which said *Hay* or *Seeds* on them.

Snap off the spigots glued hard to some display.

The ones fused into a shelf under which were all manner of concrete birdbaths which'd cost hobby gardeners a fortune.

At the Toy Store, the cheapo figures, vehicles, the knock-offs were always my favorite.

The *nothing* of them.

The *absolute*.

I wanted a toy that was simply *Space Man*.

A car that was merely *car*.

More than figures, though, on certain boxes were collectable cards, dotted lines around them, waiting to be cut out. I wanted these. Cards for generic *soldier, fireman, detective, mutant, alien, ghost*. I wanted a collection of the proof of what nobody else wanted. The full set. Wanted to *flit-flit-flit* through a stack of them. Be able to regale myself with details of their dime-a-dozen adventures, histories, hopes, failures, demises.

I wanted to show the unevenly trimmed cards to the kids at school. Children built from the ground up to disregard them. Children who'd mock me. Think me some rube who didn't know his parents could only afford the reject toys.

I wanted them to know I didn't even have the toys.

I'd snuck scissors to the store.

Removed the cards without purchase.

Taken the heart from the Idol.

I wanted them to find me peculiar.

Be never certain about me.

After appointments, my mom would sit, me beside her, with the pediatrician, arranging my next visit. The doctor's desk was littered with finger-sized, bronze statuettes. Mats of thick felt on their bases.

It wasn't so much the statuettes I wanted. I couldn't really make out what they were. After all these years I come up blank when trying to hazard a guess.

What I wanted was their *weight*. Their *thump*. The sound of the felt's cushioned impact to desktop.

The statuettes were gifts from this patient or that.

They meant something to the doctor.

I understood this.

But nothing they might mean could've meant more than that possible *thwap* to curled palm meant to me. The *thud* to the cold of the wall by my bed.

I'd watch *Mister Rogers*. Plot to steal the replicas of the buildings from the Land of Imagination which were on shelves in his kitchen, displayed behind him while he fed the fish.

If I were a guest in his home I'd shove one under my shirt.

I'd run.

In an episode of *Sesame Street*, a girl bought some bubbles. She tore them free from a length of cardboard. Cut them from the green fishnet packaging they hung in. Explained to the camera how wasteful the packaging was. All she'd wanted was the bubbles.

All I wanted was an empty green fishnet sack.

At the Supermarket I wanted toothpicks shaped like swords. Clear plastic. Yellow, green, blue, red.

What for?

To have. To leave places like a secret sign I'd been there. To pretend to find left by interlopers. As though coming across a code no one else understood.

I wanted a box of colored pasta. Bowties. Green, beige, red, purple. Not to eat. To listen to the shake of. Listen to the tinkle of their pour. To count into piles. Plant in the soil like seeds I knew wouldn't grow.

Every time we left the Pizzeria, I'd stare out the car window the entire drive home. Head soupy with how much I'd wanted one of the ashtrays. Or a disembodied joystick from the arcade machine. Even just its bulbous top. The *Fire* button. The *Jump*. To close one in each hand like rare coins pickpocketed.

At the Department Store I fixated on the elevator. Its main button. Going down. Going up. The green triangle's *bing* before the rattle of the sliding doors opening beneath it. Inside the stale cubicle I'd dream of being able to swipe the unglowing circles my mom pressed alight. *LL* and *UL*.

The measuring devices for shoe-size intoxicated me. I could almost taste their metallic. Could see myself having absconded with one. Hiding it out in some bushes. Going to it to measure my feet. My hands. My knees. My elbows.

I wanted a wallet. Or rather wanted the fake credit cards, IDs inside the ones for sale.

Wanted the images which came with picture frames. To fill up a binder with them.

But most of all, while my mom shopped for clothes, I wanted the buttons from button-flies or those which decorated the sleeves of certain coats. Wanted the rivets from the rear pockets of jeans. Wanted zippers from slacks or the sides of ankle boots.

Just zippers.

A zipper and a free floating length of linen.

Of leather.

Denim.

Houndstooth.

I recall the desire for these fragments most especially. Because it at least made sense to me they were valued. A coat would be marked deficient by the absence of such accoutrement. Not because it couldn't close proper, but because its finest part was missing. The pants wouldn't diminish in price because they were damaged, but because they'd lost what they were.

Everyone wanted buttons, rivets, zippers. Were willing to pay money, don garments because they figured it was the only way to get at these jewels.

At piano lessons I'd ache to steal the cloudy pearl bulb atop the metronome. The one that blinked orange. Orange the color of slaked thirst. That bulb and its *blink*. Whichever mechanism in the guts of the stocky black box called out *tsk-tsk-tsk*. The sound, the sight. The only reason for music was to want them.

If I could, I'd steal the hammer of the keyboard's lowest *D*. Lay at night on my back, tapping it to my forehead. Hearing the dull bump of my boogeyman tune.

I DON'T KNOW HOW OR for what I was given the forty dollars. But I had it. Two sterling twenties. Courtesy my mom. A reward. For something.

What?

I'd accomplished a commendable deed, I suppose.

But no matter how I strain to recollect, all these years a lump between then and now, the memory simply isn't in me of having done anything civic.

I had a head scratcher on my hands. That I recall. An acute affliction of sudden affluence.

Now that I had this boodle, what to do with it?

What was it good for?

My ambition stalled out, at an absolute loss.

Spend it?

I figured this went without saying.

Not all at once, maybe. Spend a bit because I could, though. I was a champion or a model citizen or whatever I was that'd earned me the dough, after all. Indulge a bit. For the principle.

There were moments I specifically considered buying some item or another I'd previously thought to steal. I could obtain many a trinket. I could purchase, relative to my age and station, something quite substantive.

No barriers.

Mom or dad would take me wherever I wanted to go.

No cloak-and-dagger, not a touch of skullduggery required to get me to a cashier.

I'd be the boss.

But the thought of tendering the money across made the money feel like *money* to me. The items being given me in exchange for it made them seem merely *items*.

Spending money for items lacked romance, put simply. It got me things yet seemed to lack getting me the things I wanted.

Plus, I already got the things I wanted. In the common parlance. My folks were more than generous.

I had toys which brought me abiding joy. More joy than most toys to most children. The time I spent enjoying the playthings I was gifted with regularity through the kindness of my parents during the course of my childhood were integral to how I wiled away the days.

Games with action figures and die-cast metal cars were sagas lasting weeks.

Comic books were read and reread and reread.

I never lacked for paper, pencil, pen, crayon, magic marker.

There was the television, more entertainment available through it than I could ever exhaust.

Not to mention videogames which fascinated me and were explored, plumbed, made into extensions of lived experience more than any designer could have ever intended.

The disembodied money I held, the notion of relinquishing it, perturbed me. I couldn't shake the feeling that though I'd be receiving something, more gravely I'd be giving something away.

There wasn't any sagacity to my fiscal cold feet. No tycoon savviness. I didn't mean some future security was at hazard or else that I more valued the ability to grant myself a later pleasure by showing restraint in the immediate.

I meant in the pure terms.

Giving something to get something just *got* something.

Got something and lost the ability to *get* something.

Codified, somehow, the hierarchy of *want* and *get* and *got*.

There was no pulse to any of it. Such *wanting*. Such *getting*. Such *having*. Nothing to build up a personalized steam of excitement behind.

Just an act. Like urination.

Pleasure to drink something. Pleasure to void myself. Pleasure to depress a flush lever.

But for what?

It was a process that happened. The pleasure automatic. Involuntary.

Money was so of the world.

The world everyone dwelt in.

The world I didn't find interesting and every day felt more apart from than a part of.

There was nothing curious about money. The most straightforward, uncreative concept.

Work to get some.

Have it.

Use it for stuff.

Or else 'Here's a gift of some. Lucky you, to have some in hand you hadn't needed to work for.'

Use it.

Get stuff.

Enjoy.

I had nothing against that principally.

The trouble was it was boring to think about. Nothing clever or intricate to understand. I learned nothing about myself or the world.

It was more fun to think about general ways *having the money* could be extended. *Spending* while still *retaining*. The amount lessened, but the *It* not.

Each time I spent some, the dial could be reset to I hadn't.

With thirty bucks left, it'd be easy enough to tell myself 'Say you'd only been given thirty to begin with.'

Twenty. Fifteen.

Ten nine eight.

Zero.

Right where I'd started.

What was the matter with that?

How many portions could it be divvied into?

One dollar per-day for forty days.

Five dollars every weekend for two months, so sixty days.

Find some kind of habit to cultivate. An enjoyment.

Buy a pack of gum. Chew a stick each evening.

A dollar plonked to buy each pack. Twenty sticks to a pack. Gum to last a year.

Make gum my trademark. Leave wads of it places. Little evidences of myself which could be episodes to others. Stepped on. Scraped to pavement squares in annoyance. Left on bookstore shelves for staff members to pick up. Workers having to soap cherry or spearmint fragrance from their fingertips before continuing their duties.

But that was as much fun to *think about* as to *do*.

More fun to think about.

Everything was such a yawn to *do*.

My mom pointed out how there was no need to spend the

money right away. Or at all. Gave the typical 'Start a college fund' style parental bromides. Only more clever than most of those. My mom was always more clever than most of everything.

My older brother had ideas. Mathematiced the windfall out for me so I didn't need to bother my head with it.

We could be a team. He the idea-man. I the stake-horse.

Think of the snacks we could buy, for example. A single twenty could get $X$ boxes of fruit roll-ups plus $X$ number of brownies plus $X$ cans of soda and so forth.

I could stash it all in our shared basement room.

Think about that, eh?

Every night we could listen to the radio while munching away.

My brother had another idea, too.

After all, I had a lucky forty dollars. Twenty could get us flush with cookies and cola for ages. No need to throw down the whole spread on the snack enterprise.

If I couldn't think of how to spend the remainder, why not kick in twenty of it to his 'Get Edvard more *Ninja Turtles* fund'?

He'd had his eyes on copies of the original Eastman and Laird issues. Each costing a pretty penny. With my contribution, he could procure nearly the entire set.

This appealed to me.

His suggestion and his proposition.

I mulled it all over.

It was nice to think my brother would owe me something. Not the money back. Nothing that had a name. An abstraction. Something I had no means of getting from him and which likely wouldn't be forthcoming.

It tickled me, too, how it was *twenty dollars* he was trying to finagle. Considering our history.

Snacks?

Sure. I could get behind that. But only in a vague kind of way.

Set us up a pantry of treats. A secret stash.

I cared less about eating them than the idea of curating the wooden chest we'd store them in.

Really liked the thought of opening the boxes containing six individually wrapped pairs of fudge brownies. Stacking them. Lining up the beverage cans. Looking down at the cache. Counting the objects. Knowing how many I ate. Seeing how many my brother would get at versus me.

Was it something I needed to ask permission to do, buying snacks, keeping them in my room?

Or was the money mine to dispense with as I saw fit?

That was the idea of having cash, was it not?

To experience a sensation. A mastery of the universe.

Would that be acceptable? I asked my mom, laying out the whole snack schematic.

She told me 'No.'

I didn't get her drift.

She explained I could buy snacks, surely. It was my money, so if I wanted to she'd let me fritter it that way. But her tone betrayed there'd be some disappointment if things broke in such direction.

Also, she didn't want me to cede to my brother's will on the *Ninja Turtles*.

I'd be making a mistake.

The money was mine.

I'd earned it somehow.

He hadn't done anything to deserve it.

As to the snacks, if I bought them I'd have to eat them according to the established rules of the house. 'In which case' she pointed out 'why buy them?' She already got snacks for my brother and I.

This was a solid point.

It was also quite vexing.

The truth was, money forced me into make-believe not of my making. I had the dough I had, but had to spend it according to

dictates external. Or else I'd have to invent some whimsical desire which would merely appear my own.
　Seem what a *kid would want*.
　What was *acceptable*.
　Was nothing to do with me.
　Having money kept me from being a thief. That was its design.
　So I did give twenty to my brother.
　He had his *Ninja Turtle* issues.
　I bought snacks.
　Ate them only when I shouldn't have.

STEALING MY FRIEND'S *POUND PUPPY* was nerve wracking, out-of-body, and simplicity itself.
　Myself, my older brother, a few others were all in my friend's main floor living room.
　The place was lit like the inside of a turned sideways cereal box.
　Or so I recall it. Darker the more inside one ventured. That impression sticks with me. A slant to the light just like that.
　The whole location seems inaccurate to recall.
　It couldn't have been lit that way, because it had windows at both ends. Open curtains. I recall the dust-mote illumination through the pollen laced panes while some friends sat on the sofa, some laid on bellies on the floor.
　I recall, improperly, small lamps on end-tables giving off Sulphur glow, bruise colored.
　But this is absolutely wrong.
　I know the row house was square, not rectangle. Know I left out the front door, not the back. Because we were upstairs, not downstairs.
　I know all of that.
　Yet I know how it seemed, even more.

Everyone but me was preoccupied playing *Rygar* on the *Nintendo*, listening to *Weird Al Yankovic*, generally yucking it up.

No one but me cared about the *Pound Puppy*.

Least of all my friend whose property it was.

The *Pound Puppy* was a soft khaki color. Khaki close to pencil-shading's grey.

I knew I wanted it as soon as I saw it.

Once I touched it, there was no going back.

It was neither soft nor not-soft. Its size was perfect. For a fake dog. For a stuffed toy. For something-to-take. Yes. It was exactly the shape and density of something-to-take.

My first step was tucking it into the waistband of my pants.

I then took position, belly-down on the carpet, looking in the direction of the videogame on the television screen.

Every sensation in the world focused on the pinpoint of my spongy flesh pressing down through the stuffed dog to the hard floor beneath the carpet. I remember the images shooting through my head as I wriggled. Images of the unpolished rough of the wood beneath the vacuumed fibers. Even as I think back, these images announce themselves. Gargantuan. As though I was granted the perception of an electron microscope by my deed. Its lens the pressure of my pubis through the stiff of this stolen plush toy.

It took all my nerve to stand.

I'd no doubt I seemed suspicious in every gesture.

Why was I there, in the first place?

Why had I laid down?

Why was I standing?

A simple glance would alert someone to the *Pound Puppy* being gone. They'd have noticed it as surely as I had upon arrival. Would give a 'Hey, wasn't there a dog there when I came in?' The friend who owned it would perk up, say prideful 'My *Pound Puppy*, yeah.'

The air would go bad.

I'd be a rabbit buried down its own burrow.

I couldn't trust my upright posture to not give the game away. The lump of my theft was too apparent. So I acted out tummy ache, asked while doubled-over if I could use the bathroom.

Explored as many angles of myself as I could in the mirror glass.

Needed the plan I should've already made.

Was it better to stash the dog at my hip, put my hands down my pockets, casually announce I was heading home?

Or to stow it at the base of my back so that when I gave my 'I'm not feeling too good' farewell my usual front would be friend-facing, no different looking than ever?

Or was it best to keep it in front, lean to the doorframe while speaking my goodbye, so my regular back would be the only thing anyone could see while I left?

The hundred-million ways it could go wrong occurred to me only at that far-too-late time.

The mother overhearing. Approaching with concern. Hand to my forehead. An impromptu physical exam.

A friend waiting outside the toilet door when I exited. Giving me a paly tickle. Feeling the hidden dog. The playful action jostling it loose.

My brother saying he'd walk home with me. Squinting every few paces. So close in he'd note something amiss which would've gone unremarked from a distance.

Even if some kid said 'You'd better lay down' I'd lack the strength to resist.

Pictured the friend who owned the puppy insisting on lending me pajamas. Walking me to his room.

None of those things happened.

What did?

No one cared.

I recall vaguely someone saying 'Goodbye' after I waved. Nothing more.
Then I was outside.
My own house was a clear shot across parking lot. But I started off in the opposite direction. Through the tree-lined back area of the friend's house.
I made a preposterous circuit of the neighborhood, stuffed animal still hidden. Hobbled along like Quasimodo. Certain some kindly old woman gardening would see me. Insist on taking my temperature. Having me wait in her kitchen for my mom to come fetch me.
Sunlight mercilessly followed me. Leaned on me. Imping me. Waiting always up ahead, exactly where I'd go.
I turned what could've been a one minute trek into a half-hour ordeal.
The inside of my house smelled sweet of the churning dishwasher when I arrived. My ears were ringing and cotton stuffed.
I made immediately for a bulbous wicker basket beside the piano, beneath a living room window. A basket which came up to my hip and was filled with decorative pillows.
I pulled the *Pound Puppy* from my pants. Rummaged to the bottom of the pillow basket. Wedged the beast there. Snagging the soft flesh of my thumb side on the uneven sharp of the basket's weave, in the process. Drawing a chicken-peck of blood.
That was the last I ever knew of the *Pound Puppy*.
After stashing it, I immediately exited the house. Out the door of the basement my brother and I shared as our bedroom.
I walked farther away from my backyard than I ever had on my own. More than a mile. Maybe more than two. Out along the still fields dotted with comely shared garden spots, lined with tall unkempt grass which threatened of ticks and burrs and animal droppings.
I strolled medicine-headed past backyards enclosed within

wood gating and metal hinged wooden doors. Out past the furthest playground in the development. Into a long, blank area where suddenly there were massive metal towers draped in power-lines and the trees never had leaves. A bizarre place where sharp brambles covered a length of diamond fencing cordoning off the wealthier development which nudged into the limits of the world which was mine.

It seemed suddenly dusk, though was the same middle afternoon it had been.

I like to think I stood in that ugly field until dusk came proper. Until the sunlight discolored as the daub of its bulb fell and was gulped by the horizon line.

But it remained idle afternoon.

Remained not the way my memory holds it.

I tottered back-and-forth as though no place. Regarded the sky and breathed in deeply as though breathing in deeply was the thing to do now.

I sat to the dirt.

Laid.

Stood when there were too many lively anthills.

Stared at the wooden fences of some houses I'd always known were right where they were but felt I was sighting for the first time.

People where there were no right to be people.

Civilization where I'd come to disappear.

It is with uncanny accuracy I recall the content of my thoughts, then. Thoughts thought as like I were giving a speech of explanation to accusers who would let me go if I worded everything just so.

It was all so deliriously pleasant.

My ideas.

Myself.

The hidden and unnecessariness of all there was to me.

First, I recall explaining how I'd no use for the *Pound Puppy*. Let me be clear. No desire to play with it. Wanted nothing of the sort. Idiots.

I recall it was with umbrage I went off on a tangent how playing with stuffed animals, acting as though by magic my imagination could make them seem alive, wasn't for me, thanks all the same. Was feverish to explain my point and my disdain for being pegged as someone like that. Seethed in pedantic detail how I remembered trying to pretend my own stuffed animal was alive, once-upon-a-time. A stuffed bear. Had dressed it in a shirt. How unsatisfying it'd been. The object not talking but me working to convince myself it was. Was alive and my good friend like the tiger was to the kid in my favorite cartoon strip. Knowing it wasn't real, alive, or my friend.

I recalled in exhausting detail to my imagined interrogators the failure of such pretending. The disappointment I'd discovered in the reality of unreality.

'Why did you steal it, then?' I next imagined my mom asking me after imagining I'd been made to trek the parking lot, return the purloined toy to the mother of the heartbroken friend I'd so baldly betrayed. Recall imagining her asking me 'Since you'd no plans for it, why not just imagine stealing it? If stealing means nothing, isn't pretending-to-steal all the same?'

I hated how she'd asked this.

How I'd pretended she had. Hated learning in this manner how I obviously thought she'd not know better. Knew no better. Would ask, really, if given the chance.

'The problem' I told my mom who wasn't there and wasn't asking me anything 'is that imagination is worthless. Imagination is imaginary.'

Could she not understand how I didn't want what was pretend to not be pretend?

I didn't want to pretend I had the things with which to pretend.

I wanted them and wanted to know myself sat there pretending with them.

'I thought you didn't want to pretend' my mom didn't say, slow, confused, exactly how she would've said had she.

No. I wanted to *be pretending*.

I didn't *want the Pound Puppy*.

I wanted *to have stolen the Pound Puppy*.

Not to *pretend I'd stolen the Pound Puppy*.

Wanted to know I was *the person who'd stolen the Pound Puppy*.

Wanted to *pretend* to be *the person who hadn't stolen the Pound Puppy*.

To be *the person pretending he wasn't the person who stole the Pound Puppy*.

I wanted to know *that* was the person I *am*.

So I'd needed to be the person I was.

.3.

I WANTED WHAT I COULDN'T have. Better. I wanted what didn't exist. To steal what didn't exist.
    Unable to do so, thwarted by my very existence, all there was was to steal what did.
    I was no philosopher. Just a thief.
    Needed no philosophy to justify myself.
    Needed no justification. Just needed things.
    These things being incidental.
    Simply the means to my having stolen.
    Which is all I wanted. To *have stolen*.
    The act of stealing was necessary to that. It was only because there was no way to circumvent this fact that I stole. Could I honestly have said I'd *stolen* without needing to *steal* I would've.
    I wasn't in charge of reality, though.
    Just subject to it.
    Lying was part-and-parcel to theft, oftentimes, and not at all pleasurable. I'd no desire to lie. Least of all to myself. The entire concept was unseemly and disheartened me. But like a cramp or a burn which athletes might speak of, there was no need to buck against it, wish it away.
    Lying was the evidence that something had been accomplished.
    Every interaction in my sanctioned life became partway a lie

due to the experiences in my unsanctioned one. This abundance of deception made it easier to treat subterfuge as a regrettable but necessary part of my constitution.

Duplicity as basecoat.

*Stealing*. The most certain thing about it, an impression I recall was quite potent to me even back then, was that it never felt clever.

*Cleverness* was another lie.

*Feeling clever* was something people who weren't thieves thought thieves did.

The uncleverness of it all, the dumbness, how rudimentary it was made me the happiest.

It was obvious everyone knew how to steal. No special hand had touched me. I was doing nothing others might envy. They'd be, all of them, right to *tsk-tsk* me. To point out the umpteen faults in my actions.

I took pleasure knowing people would think I thought I was being smart if and when they learned what I got up to. Liked how they'd be wrong. How I knew something they didn't know. Something which, if I told them, would come off as flippancy.

The truth is: I thought I was being an imbecile.

A reckless, lovelorn little dolt.

I wasn't old enough yet to walk to a nearby Shopping Center. All for the best. The very fact I wasn't supposed to go there allowed me to disguise I'd been doing so and, consequently, left me never having to worry my parents would suspect me of stealing from its stores.

Anyone wondering where I was of a day would assume I was 'outside'. Roaming the development's vast fields. Down at the creek.

For most of the day, most days, they'd be correct.

If I were apprehended at the Shopping Center it'd be an unmitigated disaster. Such tension gave the act of traveling so that I might steal a mystique, in itself. This forbiddenness of place supplied a jazzy engine to the romance of my thefts.

Also, the set-up allowed me the prefect doorway to step in-and-out of.

On this side: I was who people knew me as.

On that side: I was who I was.

From an Art Supply Store I'd swipe sketchbooks. The most aesthetically pleasing kind. Small. Thick, rough covers.

Sometimes I'd nab canvases the same size as the sketchbooks. Smaller ones, too.

I'd steal charcoals and pastels to go with.

I was no artist. Didn't fill the sketchbooks more than a few pages each, displeased with anything I'd render. Though it was always a pleasure setting down the doodles. Even putting some solid work into them.

My dirty hands after rendering on canvas gave me terrific joy. Thumb-sides thick in charcoal soot and oil paste. The smudges my touch would smear because I'd leave my hands unscrubbed could be found everywhere.

It was the process, the nuts-and-bolts of theft which entertained me.

How to poke through the soft cardboard backs of the packs of charcoals, pastels, or pens.

Slip the items out.

Get them to pocket.

Stash the gutted wrappings away.

The little playacts performed to give the impression to any possible observer I was comparing some item to some other while really I was secreting sketchbooks to waistline or to coat pocket.

Savvy shopper, I'd seem. A lad who knew what he wanted but was bred clever enough to price compare.

It was the same with stealing models of starships.

I could care less for the finished products, but the bits-and-pieces, waiting in all their blank grey majesty to be snapped off the plastic matrixes which housed them, were exquisite.

The decals. A desire for these was almost delirium. Knowing I was stealing something called a *decal* was enough to make it absurd to do anything but.

I'd have to steal liquid cement, also.

Expensive glass bottles of specialized paint.

So much fun using fingernails to zip through the soft plastic covering the boxes of the models. Fingernails, again, or else a sharp item I'd borrow from some other aisle used to slice the boxes' underbellies. Get at the five-hundred, one-thousand, two-thousand itty-bitty pieces. Slip them into a bag I'd brought with.

I adored burying the hollowed boxes back behind the still vital ones. Loved checking for weeks after to find the carcasses hadn't yet been discovered.

I never stole the instructions for the replica kits. For love nor money I'd not be able to sleuth out how to properly assemble the models without them, of course. Didn't have the slightest desire to.

I glued together spacecraft of my own lazy design. My index and third finger would always wind up fused together from the industrial adhesive.

It isn't to say there came no pleasure at all in possessing the items I stole. Theft, truth be told, led to some very distinct enjoyments in ownership.

The things.

Having them.

Having what was in the things.

What could be taken from them.

A rarified treat. Indulgence impossible otherwise. Gratification like from touching stiches binding a wound. From caressing the odd thickness of scar tissue. Very worth the laceration despite the world-at-large would recommend against getting cut.

From the Drugstore I'd once wandered with my mom's purloined twenty dollars, impossible to spend, I now stole movies.

There was a rotating display rack of VHS offerings. All manner of films, most of which bored me immensely to contemplate. But there were cassettes which contained old kung-fu flick double features. A plump assortment of them. Films resplendent in grainy photography, tinny music, delicious dubbed vocals, every character probably voiced by the same performer. So delectable the sound-effects of footfalls, of punches, of kicks, of cloth flapping, swords touching, of jugulars being crumpled by the iron grips of murderous turncoats or by students of murdered masters quenching their revenge.

These films became instant loves of my life. Ingrained to my person. A pleasure derived from them akin to stretching out my legs upon waking.

Had I needed to wait to have them, had they not come from giving in to the impulse to steal, would this beloved part of my history, of my very *self,* not exist?

It's a fact how had I asked for them they wouldn't have been given me.

My dad, with his absurd abhorrence of anything violent, would've taken them away had he known I'd possessed them, nevermind agreeing to front me the price of purchase.

My mom, too, wouldn't have gleefully bought me the dozen cassettes, ten dollars a pop, I'd wound up in possession of. Even if she did buy me one, it wouldn't have been immediately upon my sighting it. I'd have had to save up. Earn the cost.

I wonder whether the movies would've imprinted on me so absolutely if I couldn't have returned to the Drugstore on a whim to pluck another then another then another, drawn feverish by my desire. To this day, I enjoy the puzzle of considering whether purchasing them with money earned or having been gifted me would've perhaps curtailed my eagerness to explore them.

Even in my enjoyment of these treasure I was picky, I admit.

Some flicks were clear favorites from first blush, remain miracles to this day.

Others were dreck, duds, dumpy little turkeys without enough action, with fights not choreographed elegantly enough. Bores. Progressions of nothingness I'd not even watch the entireties of, cast aside with a shrug.

This variance in quality was important.

As was the fact that the subpar offerings outnumbered the examples of excellence.

It was the roulette I kept going back for.

SOON ENOUGH I HAD A cohort. Alain. Together we were allowed to go to the shops. Safety in numbers. A trust extended.

This new freedom granted me was on the heels of a general allowance having been made among the neighborhood mothers that we kids were free to jaunt to buy things provided we traveled in groups. Preferably an older kid would lead the pack. A stalwart, dependable sort like my older brother.

Alain and I were a duo, only. But considering our rapport and how the majority of our time was spent only in each other's company, the exception was made by my mom that we two could trek out as we saw fit.

Provided we were together.

Alain's own mother couldn't have given a hoot where he went, so far as I ever knew. He'd been making the trip with me for ages before the blessing came down and the burden of keeping my whereabouts obscured was eased.

I hadn't had a friend all my own since third-grade. Had only known that friend while at school. In school, I'd been inseparable from him. At the end of the year, he'd moved away.

I'd never quite thought he was like me, though, that friend. For all we'd had in common and jointly enjoyed, he was a true straight-shooter with neither head nor heart for seeing life his own way. Was giddy about hitting the benchmarks, moving the designated track. Excelled in all he did. Top-of-the-class, a cinch. Sure to succeed. Won Science awards meant for high-schoolers. Would confess to the teacher he'd not worked the full half-hour on a homework assignment if it'd only taken him ten minutes, nevermind he'd aced the thing, extra-credit on top.

A wonderful pal.

But he'd no idea the nature of my mind.

Had I let him in on it, I doubt he'd have much approved.

When I'm honest with myself, I know I loved that friend more than he loved me. I knew him more than he knew me, absolutely. I'm certain I've thought of him far more often in these thirty-odd years since knowing him than he has of me. I doubt very much he recalls my name. If he does, I can't help but suppose it's with a touch of embarrassment over who he cavorted with when he was little.

I am, perhaps, his 'There, but for the grace of God, go I.'

Of course I had my older brother.

Now had a younger one, too.

The neighborhood children were all fond of me and I of them. We lived our lives in-and-out of each other's homes and company. But such friendships were communal property. However much enjoyed one of us was by any other of us individually, the bonds we had came prepackaged with living where we lived.

Nothing about these friends was exclusive to me.

Alain lived in the same housing development as the rest of us but in a neighborhood adjacent to mine.

I've no idea anymore how exactly we first became friends. One of those situations where two people are at the playground, each alone, leave together, from that point on, in school and at home, joined at the hip.

It happened fast. I do recall thinking so even as it did.

Blink.
Alain.
He and I in his basement.
We got on very well. Simpatico in most things.
Followed religiously the same contemporary cartoons, enjoyed the same videogames, the same needlessly vulgar jokes.
Worked together coming up with epic ideas for comic book series we were certain would light the world on fire.
Spent hours at his house watching the same few Anime films available to rent from the Comic Shop. Pausing at all the titillating sequences, running them slow-motion was Alain's particular bent.
At school we held the same people in bad blood and shared a generally down-our-nose opinion of whatever the common throng thought was terrific. Even when our likes gelled with the mainstream, we both were double-quick to conclude our understanding was deeper than our peers'.
We'd roam the neighborhood far-and-wide and spent days sneaking around a nearby Office Park still under construction. Rooted through the dumpsters there. Marveling at disused fax machines. Uncovering random lingerie catalogues some worker had discarded.
Alain would take one catalogue, let me take another, seeing as there tended to be multiple.
I'd have let him take them all if I hadn't thought he'd find the gesture off-putting.
It was in his basement I sliced open my knee quite dreadfully on a curve of shattered coffee cup. A wound I'd tried to keep hidden from my family but which thankfully my older brother brought to my dad's attention. A quarter-centimeter deeper, the damage would've been irreparable. I'd have a limp to this day. Two hours later to the Emergency Room, I would've required a transfusion to make up for lost blood.

Wonderful, wonderful times.

Alain was more than down for shoplifting, too. I don't even recall having to broach the concept as though a taboo. To the contrary. He was more than game for stealing whatever was on the docket.

His eagerness more than made up for the fact that I knew he was more commonplace in his desires for snatching things than myself. I liked how he was. In some ways found comfort in it. In many respects envied him.

Thoughtless theft.

Like an amoeba.

Gulped in whichever thing.

Digested it.

Ready for another.

I came to think of Alain as a *criminal*. Whereas I was a *thief*.

*Thievery* was incidental to his bent, *criminality* incidental to mine.

In my most bigheaded musings, I'd lay in bed wondering whether it was his way of existing which was soulless or was it mine.

It seemed more romantic to be soulless, so I copped to that.

Needing another word for his way of life, I went with *automaton*.

Stealing became a clockwork endeavor, a scheduled, even necessary part of a given day.

Chewing gum and oatmeal cookies and cheese puffs.

The act of obtaining these items became rote.

Where we'd stand to secret each item.

How we'd use the little bit of pocket cash one or the other of us might have handy to serve as cover. Give ourselves the appearance of regular, paying customers.

Bodies thick with swiped goods, we'd wait in line at the checkout to purchase soda, something it was tougher to steal.

The first times doing this were tense and enjoyable. My ears attuned to every unwanted crinkle from cookie packages in my waistline. It was as though the vibrations traveled through my veins and announced themselves audible out every pore. I was certain there was a notable falseness in my jocular affect with Alain, our chatter exaggerated for benefit of the clerk. I could taste my breath. My vision clouded as though from chlorine after submerging in pool water. It was doubtless something about me would be enough excuse for an adult to insist on having the both of us stand to one side to be pat searched.

Before too long, there was no nervousness whatsoever.

I could forget I even had items on me there'd be no explanation for if discovered.

Any notion of what would happen were Alain or I caught out stopped crossing my mind.

We got flamboyant in how much we'd make off with each day. Would leave the Drugstore. Walk to some nearby bushes to unload our goodies. Traipse to another store where we'd take a haul of whatever was our aim there. Stash that stuff. Return to the Drugstore for another lift of snacks.

Only when it got boring or it was time to get home to watch a cartoon would we gather everything up in old plastic grocery bags we'd brought to keep in the hidey-hole

A day wasn't complete without a trip to the stores.

Without our leaving bloat with boodle the bulk of which was discarded on the walk home for lack of having a way to explain its presence to our parents.

What most endeared me to Alain was the perfunctory, nonchalant way he'd give a swing and an underhand toss of the bagful of our day's accomplishments to land it in a dumpster we'd pass on the walk home. No thought for the items inside. Not a concern to stock up or actually go through with other ways to profit we might've invented.

Resell the candy at school.
Use it to endear ourselves to whomever.
I don't know what kick Alain got, just knew it wasn't the same kick I did. Which made it more interesting.
His life had no reflection, just function.
Mine had no function, but reflection in spades.
We became thick, Alain and I.
Not quite as-thieves, but near it.


AS OUR KNACK FOR BEING jolly little bandits grew, so grew thoughts of intricate schemes, capers, undertakings far more difficult than snatch-and-go.

Such musings were, for me, another fun way of cataloguing the vast swaths of emptiness in the world. Another avenue to explore in detail the aspects of existence which someone had put thoughtful work into, had real design and purpose to them, but were meant to go unnoticed, ideally.

Apprehending so strictly the areas of life around me no one else was giving a sniff to felt like being perpetually in disguise.

The composition of stores' back office windows, for example. Managers were able to see out, but try to look in and it was only your reflection on black you'd get rewarded with, even with your nose smooshed all the way to the glass.

Sightlines from cashier counters.

Closed-circuit cameras.

Circular mirrors set at angles in corners and aisle ends.

It fascinated me to no end to reason out why certain items were placed where they were in a store over certain others.

The varying levels of defense.

The hierarchy of disposable versus would-be-a-loss-to-lose.

What were the differentiating factors between *worthy* and *worthless*?

Toasters, for example, or cord-powered eggbeaters might have magnetic strips inside their cardboard boxes, mechanisms to trip an alarm at the exit. Whereas an individual wooden ladle or a yellow plastic spatula would have no safeguards of any stripe.

A compact-disc of popular music might be encased in a shell requiring the turnkey kept around an assistant manager's neck. Whereas cassettes of music might have strips like the eggbeaters.

Such strips, however, would be unhidden.

On the outside of the cassette cases.

Precautions easily removable with the measliest peel.

A defense only mounted with a sigh by some listless worker forced to have something to do.

These differing provisions would be the case even if the compact-disc and the cassette were of the same music.

Even when the compact-disc wound up discounted below the price of the cassette.

Alain and I would work out simple tricks based on the nuances of particular establishments. We'd sometimes even come up with dialogues to recite while we made our rounds, as though performers in perpetual dress rehearsal.

Candy came in wrappers, for example. Since it mattered not what happened to said wrappers, we'd slip two or three wrapped bars into a fountain soda cup, fill it, be drinking while paying for the beverage, then out the door we'd go.

I found a folksy pleasure in coming up with low-key techniques such as those.

But I never figured they were anything more than obvious.

Everyone must figure out such pat-a-cake just from having an idle look around.

So I loved eyeballing customers in shops. Patrons at gas pumps. People waiting on buses, loitering in front of fast-food restaurants.

What were *they* up to?

Or at least what did they know they *could* be up to?

How many people other than me were pulling the exact same ploys, even smack on the very same day as I?

Had the girl leaving a bookstore as I'd entered it done, five minutes prior, exactly what I was about to do?

I wondered if the workers in a given shop, especially adult employees, knew every trick being turned, simply couldn't be bothered to get confrontational when they spotted out a likely crook.

Alain and I made guesstimates about how many clerks in whichever shop had their own under-the-table goings-on going on. We would walk for hours, eating sour candies, gulping double-caffeinated colas, trying to suss out what these plots might be.

For goodness sake, if one had a personal buddy working as the cashier of some joint it'd be simplicity itself for them to let you walk out unmolested, laden down with ill-gotten goods.

Or, to keep up appearances, they might even ring out a few of your items, acting like they didn't know you from a hole in the wall, whilst meantime you had a bagful of contraband they'd make no move to inspect.

They might even scan two-out-of-seven items you brought up to the till, tender the transaction, bag the unscanned lot alongside the legally purchased, right out in the wide open.

We wondered if businessmen, moguls merely accepted such loses as read. Chalked them up to something as unavoidable, even as necessary, as a telephone bill or the cost of air conditioning.

Want people to come in the store?

Gotta let some of 'em steal.

No shop wants to give off the vibe its livelihood depends on not coming up short the price of some peanut-butter cups.

Want people to work for you?

Let 'em take a few things a day.

Good for morale. No shift manager wants to come across like

a sheriff. Customers don't want to get a whiff of Alcatraz when they need to pop in for bismuth or a greeting card.

Once the Shopping Center we were permitted to walk to became old hat, we naturally ventured to new territory. Expanded operations.

My memory is of this being an absolutely organic development. I certainly don't recall there being any active discussion. No proposals presented, justified, assented to.

Not on my part, anyway.

Maybe Alain had conjured masterplans in his own time, initiated whichever move based on those, and I'd just drifted along, towed by his inertia when whichever day came was the first we'd do something new.

This makes sense.

I was the good little solider.

Point me where to go.

A goldfish ready to grow to the requisite size of whichever bowl. Learn its water. Its limits. Swim there in bliss until dunked someplace else.

The Supermarket was far larger than the Drugstore. We had to cross two major, multi-laned intersections to get to it.

This adventure brought with it loads of nervous excitement. A perfect, renewable anxiety. Impossible to become acclimated to the pitfalls presented. Every time, the traffic could easily be thick with snitches.

How would we explain ourselves if any adult in either of our orbits spotted us?

This same danger was present in the store's interior, in fact.

There came several occasions where only lucky chance had saved us being spied by either one or the other of my parents. Once we'd only last second spotted Alain's older sister. Three steps more and we'd have blundered right into her.

It tickled me how it differed to steal from the Supermarket than to steal from the Drugstore. How it differed to steal from the Drugstore than from the small Grog next to the Comic Shop.

For the Grog, we needed the down-home ingenuity of the soda-cup gambit and its ilk.

For the Drugstore we needed to know all manner of intricacies.

Which aisles were the most deserted but still well-traveled enough our ducking into them a quick minute when we needed to tuck something to waistband wouldn't seem odd?

Where could we temporarily stash items so they'd not be stumbled across while we collected other items to add to the pile before making one quick dump of the collected goods into the bag either of us had obtained from purchasing something legitimate before pretending to wander over to gather the other to head home?

Scrumptious complications.

But at the Supermarket we'd have had to think up preposterous challenges for ourselves to make even rudimentary precautions necessary.

There were abundant snack items to choose from we could simply eat as we walked around, no one batting an eye at us.

Doughnuts could be plucked right from the self-serve glass case, twist-tied into a bag, put on a scale to get a price label, and then eaten as we casually inspected and pocketed packs of collectable stickers from cartoons we enjoyed. The crumpled, empty bags could simply be stuffed in our pockets.

We could ask for cookies from the bakery by the half-pound. The confections would be packaged, handed to us, a price sticker printed, affixed to the box's outside. A happy worker in hat and smock would assume we were taking the parcel to our parents who'd pay for the goods up front, as required. Anyone who saw us munching away while we stood around reading magazines would figure, likewise, our parents had us waiting while they shopped, were permitting us to enjoy our sweets in the meantime.

The public bathroom being down a corridor through swinging doors allowed us to basically take our time stealing whatever we desired.

Tucked back by the Seafood Department, air thick with brine, there was no one guarding the entrance. No inspector walking in-and-out of the lavatory itself.

We would put one copy of a kung-fu magazine into another copy of itself and stroll right through the flap doors, chatting.

Shouldering then through the toilet door, we'd cloister in a stall, securing one copy of the magazine down our pants.

Were anyone monitoring a camera, we'd clearly be seen waltzing back out with the same magazine we'd gone in with.

Observed while returning it to the shelf.

It was as though the wider the world, the fuller the expanse, the more accepted was someone like me.

Theft existed invisibly.

Indistinguishable from even its opposite.

A thief's anonymity came unsolicited, unpracticed.

As an insult.

THE WALK TO THE SHOPPING Mall was a dreamscape to me.

Miles beyond the Supermarket.

A sneak under a fence behind a motel.

A walk along train tracks, two miles. Part of the honest-to-God highway grumbling beneath me. The *whoosh* of a locomotive five minutes long *chugachugging* at my shoulder, breeze of its *rattle-rattle* tousling my hair.

A venture over a road dense with traffic, six lanes thick.

Would the crosswalk, its icon in white-green indicating my turn, really protect me?

I was spectacularly where I oughtn't be.

A price on my head.

Every moment a glory.

The Shopping Mall itself, however, was a debilitating excursion into perdition.

The scope of commerce, the variety of people was a bridge too far for my sensitive little heart. I was a kid shier than an orchid. My constitution on the best of days was held together by rubber bands and chewing gum.

So many anonymous eyes on me under the constant thrum of music overhead drowned me in unease. I felt the molecules of my soul unbuckling. My skin calcified in anxiety.

In such a miasma any of these people could be a booby trap, the landmine which might explode me.

I'd never felt more unwanted. Unneeded.

I was invisible. But only the way a stomachache was.

People didn't see me.

But they noticed me.

Wanted me gone.

I was a virus the immune system of this place would work to expel.

The Shopping Center, Supermarket, were my limit.

Why not?

I didn't need any more than those places. Their conditions. Their rules.

Being myself in that world was akin to studying the details in a comic book panel, perusing the fine print of an advertisement. Materials meant for me to see. To study. To love.

This place, this mall, being alone in it, alone with Alain, was like watching a sack of spider eggs hatch. Seeing the vermin scramble on terrifyingly fresh legs all directions. It was falling into a termite den, wresting myself free, wondering how many of the louse remained on me no matter how far away I'd run after, how furiously I'd brushed at myself, washed hair, changed clothes.

It was an incessant gnarl of ludicrous light and sound.

A garbage scow.

One the size of a cruise ship.

Money made sense there.

But thievery didn't.

Stealing, as easy as it might be, was stripped of its literacy.

The opposite-of-contemplation was all that could survive in these pointless franchise boutiques.

Where was the romance?

Of course I might find things I wanted. Items I'd certainly have coveted were they found someplace else.

Movies, for example.

Here was a store, a vast warehouse of items on sale with the variety of a rental shop. Too many too many too many. So many that the choice to swipe one didn't feel a true choice. Nothing borne of desire.

Desire needed limits. A crucible to prove itself in.

Ten items to choose from, one catches your fancy, prompts you to action?

That means something.

One-hundred, five-hundred items?

A display wherein every one thing seems as worth having as any other doesn't allow choice. Only selection.

A thief couldn't curate in this environment.

All there was to be here was *consumer*.

Anything I might snatch felt random.

No treasure required a value which could only be assigned by me. There was too much abundance to allow for anything beyond 'I want that.'

*I want that.*

No *What for?*

It was as though there were no pieces, truly, to this mess. The world on display was slurry. Stealing seemed gluttonous. An act without anchor. Combine that with the grotesque bloat of the possible repercussions and it was an act of no grace.

In this environment I was no more than a sentient crumb. Pitifully vulnerable. Being caught out by whichever thoughtless authority in this glitz would eradicate me.

A call to my mom?

I was *where*?

Why?

Why was I *there*?

I'd have no honest answer to give.

Or none I'd want to admit to.

'I made a mistake' would be the truth. But no one I'd say it to would hear or give sympathy to what I meant by *mistake*.

The possibility of being apprehended didn't frightened me. It made me angry. How no logic, personality, or identity would come into play.

The world, when on the scale of Shopping Mall, seemed all a mechanism. Theft came off like it would need justification. Some rot like *Alain and I versus the world*.

Us against a world which wasn't against us.

Was merely oblivious to our existence.

A world I'd nothing against, either. Wanted no part of. Let alone combat with.

I loathed the idea of having to justify myself. But being caught at the mall would require it. Necessitate some lie.

*Rebelliousness*?

Even at ten years old I found the concept of 'rebelling' weak tea so far as a reason for anything.

*Lashing out*?

Theft shouldn't be anything such. I refused to say it was.

Theft was tinkering at a puzzle. Knowing one's heart.

But if I was caught in the godforsaken Shopping Mall, saying things like that would come off idiotic. I'd start crying.

It was the truth, but not in such a place.

Alain didn't seem to mind the mall. Happy as a clam. His mood and demeanor as unblemished as ever I'd known them.

Nor did he seem to want to steal. He was, in fact, quite content to fete on the provisions lifted from the Supermarket on the way over. Wait until the way back to grab more if still hungry.

Alain, of course, had never really wanted to steal.

Alain just would. Or Alain wouldn't.

It was all the same to him.

He merely wanted to exist for periods of time inside the Shopping Mall.

Be there.

Roam.

We'd look through shops, but why he wanted to seemed impenetrably abstract to me. He didn't seem to harbor any desire to purchase anything.

To do anything but drift.

I couldn't get on his wavelength

What kind of existence was that?

All the risks merely for the privilege of sitting in a wobbly chair at the Food Court?

Though for Alain, I wondered: Was there risk?

On walks home, relieved, free from the bacon pop of strangers' eyes all over me, faceless eyes like hypodermics missing the vein missing the vein missing the vein, I'd burst alive. *Rat-tat-tat* would blast out all kinds of clever ideas I'd come up with for capers. I'd no desire to enact the plans. Knew we wouldn't. Words just needed to flow from me. I needed to feel close to Alain. Conceal my disquiet.

He's be convivial enough as I'd gab about some plot. Chummy and buoyant while I laid out the stakes like Prime Time.

The Movie Store had state-of-the-art alarm klaxons, flagrantly on display as a deterrent at the wide mouth of its entrance.

Every VHS had sensors wedged inside the cardboard of the art boxes, underneath the shrink wrap.

Fifty people around at all times. Employees. Customers.

No possibility of cutting the plastic, slipping out the cassettes, chucking the boxes unseen. Besides, I was pretty certain the dome mirrors on the ceilings were cameras.

What a delightful chess puzzle, Alain would agree. He'd listen to the blabber of my mind which couldn't stop its churn, its chatterbox need to outwit these obstacles on principle alone.

My plan would necessitate the two of us working in an intricate tandem.

We'd enter separately and wouldn't interact.

Alain would get the item we aimed to steal into a bag.

We'd hang around a bit, looking at this, that, or the other.

Alain then starts heading toward the door.

I do likewise, some few steps behind.

But I have an absentminded air, looking at a movie box I am still holding.

Alain and I get to the sensor at the same moment.

It blares its outrage.

I immediately recoil, stepping back, holding up the movie I have in hand and making profuse apologies, sheepishly backpedal into the store.

Alain meantime has kept walking.

I hang out awhile longer.

Eventually leave empty handed.

No alarms sound.

Alain applauded and laughed at the pluckiness. But then he talked some rubbish about how aluminum foil could be used to block the alarm receptors from responding to the sensors. According to him, we could line a bag with said foil, load things into it, saunter on out.

Where had he heard this?

Who did he know who'd pulled off a scheme like that?

I didn't ask. Wanted to save him the embarrassment.

Didn't want him to have an answer. Learn he spent time with another companion.

When would he have met them?

How could he have?

Before long I concocted some story to beg off going along on the trips to the mall. Claimed a neighbor had seen me on the roadside. Grassed to my mom about it. I was in bad trouble.

'The neighbor' I said 'told my mom I was with someone else.'

Said she'd guessed Alain but I promised him I'd not confirmed the supposition. He didn't need to worry. My mom wouldn't tell his mother.

'It's okay' he told me 'my mother doesn't care'.

As for my not going the mall?

That was fine, too.

Neither would he. 'It's boring there, anyway.'

.4.

I DESIRED A HISTORY. Desired a kinda sordid one. Nothing too awful. Some checkers to me, just. Enough to develop a genuine point-of-view.

I wanted dimensions.

To be a cipher. A Rorschach.

Tilting toward the proverbial negative only made sense. Transgression is where gradations which weren't simply gratuitous would come from.

How to compare one righteous act or quality to another without coming off self-righteous, after all?

On the other hand, of scoundrels I'd heard 'What they did was bad, but it's not like they …' often enough to know every individual kept their own counsel about them.

I remember trying to come to grips about good people. Righteous people. How they seemed so blasé.

For such people to lack nuance made sense, though.

They were good, that's that. Righteous. A lack of moral variance was their polka-dot.

I already couldn't be good, of course. Righteous. Nevermind I'd no interest in being.

Didn't want to be profligate, either. Bad. Such absolutes were a snooze.

To be known as a creature of nuance wasn't entirely in my

hands, however. Life had to curate such occasion. Happy accident determined how one was seen in the eyes of their countrymen.

I could only hope to land on the manufacture of a dubious reputation by continuing to ply my trade.

Refining my talent.

Except the more I refined my talent, the less chance I'd get caught.

The less chance I'd get caught, the less hope for a wounded name.

I'd have my theft-riddled history, sure.

Which no one'd know peep about.

No one knowing made defunct the efforts of living.

Even were I to admit certain things to the public quite baldly it'd undercut me. If people only had my word to take, I was little different than some loudmouth making things up to front-off.

Besides, a thief who wasn't studied at keeping his own deeds under wraps wasn't a thief anyone would much think a thief.

Rumor.

That's what I needed.

Little spores of information dusted about.

Innuendo folks could fondle. Add elaborations to. Outright falsify.

Phantom accounts of my antics which could aim to vilify or glorify, dependent on the whim of the gossip. Would succeed or not, based on the mood of the crowd.

I recall well how this sophistic game triggered much intellectual delight in my sixth-grade mind.

It seemed of tremendous value to land on some spiritual middle-ground.

I couldn't doctor up the circumstances which might make the scandal sheets. Couldn't put the first whisper in the first ear on purpose.

I could just court the conditions which most allowed for controversy.

I'd have to continue operating in plain sight.

In an environment where I was known.

Revisiting the scenes of my crimes.

Time-after-time.

Hiking over to that garish Shopping Mall didn't add to the challenge of theft, after all. A carnival duck-shoot, reset each time it went round. I'd no doubt if I were caught stealing there I could slip on a different shirt, walk back in ten minutes after getting the boot.

Likewise, truffling out oddball hunting grounds didn't lend texture to my mystique. In fact, it lessened the potency of my potential capture.

Firstly, were I apprehended shoplifting from some store miles away, I might be let off with a slap on the wrist. No call to my parents, even. Simply turned out on my ear.

Banned from a place I'd no place to be in the first place, even less had an inkling to ever return to.

Secondly was the fact that the far flung nature of where I'd be caught would serve to make what I'd done seem a preposterous one-off to my parents if they were informed.

Here was their second born, running off to play crook. Learnt his lesson, no doubt.

My mom and dad would be the end of any tabloid footprint. They'd likely not even tell my brothers what'd gone down.

But if I were cuffed on my home turf?

That'd work a trick.

Word would spread amongst store staff, certainly. 'Keep an eye on that kid'.

Hearsay of my suspiciousness would seep through the high-school crowd who'd take note how clerks seemed to regard me with squints.

These chance observations would trickle down to kids my age by virtue of familial relations.

Spread around school based on friend-groups and the like.

Bug snug back in the nook of my Shopping Center, I vowed to appreciate the good thing I had going for me.

It was all I ever needed. My postage stamp of existence.

Here I was a fixture. Like in a television show.

A background character who might develop into a fan-favorite over enough episodes.

Being established, well known in an environment, was of paramount importance.

Because there were some rules to it all.

For example, Alain and I would never think of stealing from the Comic Shop. Those were our friends in there. Had our loyalty. We might admit how easy it'd be to make off with whatever, but would both right away and insistently reaffirm our vow that we weren't the kind of people who'd go through with such treachery.

The rub was, I was so accustomed to these home waters I'd have to manufacture ways to make them choppy.

Only three methods I could figure might accomplish this.

Break my own rules.

Steal things I truly had no desire for.

Or start trying to steal what I could already steal via superficial new methods.

The first was stupid.

The second would get me rims from the Automotive Store? No thanks.

The third made at least a semblance of sense.

Luckily, that scenario I'd concocted for stealing movies at the mall had started a sub-track going in my mind.

Such thoughts were largely impractical. I treated them like a sketchbook.

Fictions. Not life.

Silly business. Nonsense probably not physically possible.
Go to a Movie Rental Store.
Use a screwdriver to open the VHS cassettes.
Remove the spools of film.
Replace the innards of a recordable VHS I had at home with them.
Nothing I'd try. Just fun to imagine the world in such ways.
But say I made some effort to merge that track with the track of stealing things I wanted?
From the Bookstore I'd become fond of swiping paperbacks I liked the covers of.
Nothing to it.
To the trusty old waistline of my pants they'd be fit.
But how about getting creative?
Dog-ear a novel.
Write my name in it.
Highlight some passages.
Add notes here-and-there.
Walk out.
If stopped, the book'd look secondhand, already mine.
Or else I could waltz right up to the cashier. Ask if he had other books by the same author. Show my vandalized paperback with an adhesive I'd stripped from a school library book now stuck to its back.
Or how about instead of such sleight-of-hand I work to concoct a clever spy gadget?
Imagine being pat searched, even having my bag rifled through, yet walking away clean despite having a bunch of loot on me.
I'd picked up the habit of eating hard pretzels from my older brother. These came in stately cardboard boxes.
How about I open a box carefully from the bottom. Empty two-thirds of the pretzels out. Insert a false bottom which kept the remaining pretzels in the top-third of an otherwise empty shell.

I could use adhesive strips to allow me to close the box bottom's two flaps after loading in merchandise without giving them the appearance they'd ever been tampered with.

Even if someone were to inspect the pretzel box, give it a shake, it'd look and sound the way it ought to.

I built such a mechanism.

Utilized it only twice.

It was more nerve-wracking to get the stuff into the box, the box back into my bag, than it would've been to rob the joint at gunpoint.

I tried to convince myself that despite its unwieldiness, the box's clever protection made it worthwhile.

Tried to tell myself the point was to be *innovative*.

The point was to accomplish something others had accomplished but in a niftier way.

It was a tough sell.

Both times, although I wasn't caught, I felt like a nincompoop not Thomas Edison.

The box wasn't necessary.

In private moments, I lay abed picking apart the device's more ludicrous aspects.

It was superfluous. Taking something I knew I could already accomplish nimbly and adding obstructions. Trying to purport to myself that manufacturing difficulties, overcoming them, made my accomplishment somehow superior to someone else's who'd not burdened themselves so.

It'd be one thing to go from painting to painting blindfolded.

From juggling to juggling chainsaws.

Without an audience to leave gobsmacked, however, what was I playing at?

I'd heard tell of promotional madmen from olden days. Swaggering charlatan's out for a quick buck. Carnival barkers come to town who would stage boxing matches, man-against-octopus.

I didn't want to stage boxing matches against octopus.
If anything, I wanted to be an octopus.
One that landed a knockout blow.

OBLIVIOUS TO MY PSYCHIC FRUSTRATIONS, Alain put forward a proposition. Happy chance, he'd come up with precisely the prescription for what ailed me. I was embarrassed not to've landed on the solution myself.

The adult mags. At the Shopping Center Bookstore.

Why not have a go at making off with a bunch of those?

An intoxicating challenge.

The logistics of effectively undertaking the snatches thick with pitfalls.

The severity of the consequences for failure unquestionable.

Factor in the certainty our names'd become infamous were we pinched and there was no way in good conscience I could nix the idea.

Indeed, here was a danger I'd be hypocrite to balk in the face of.

No doubt Alain would take the chance on his own if I didn't join in.

Could I face myself in the mirror if he was successful while I'd sat things out?

If he let someone in on what he'd done, my name a mere footnote, I'd never live it down.

It nauseated me to contemplate my epithet.

*Coward.*

Worse.

*The guy who's too chicken for titties.*

Good God, if it became common knowledge I'd shirked this adventure people would disbelieve stories of things I had done. At best, all my past accomplishments would be reduced to quaintness. Kid games.

Any time someone asked me was it true I hadn't helped Alain in this affair and I'd float some old war story, desperate to save face, it'd come off as overcompensation.

My days would be lived out as nothing more than a *Yeah-but*.

An exile too ghastly to entertain.

With such existential spurs prodding me, I fell headlong into the task.

The magazine rack at the Bookstore consisted of a lower level and an upper. Upper level and lower each had magazines spread along six step-like tiers. Only the magazines on the lowest tier of each level could be seen full face. Everything but the titles of the offerings on the higher tiers obscured by the height of the mags on tiers below.

The skin mags occupied the highest two tiers of the rack's upper level. A dozen slots across, each tier. Twenty odd periodicals on offer. Five or six copies of each title. A lot of the mags weren't flippable without purchase. Came sealed inside of crinkly shrink-wrap. Black blocking-boards covered the face of each item, titles of the publications displayed on these blockers in generic white stencils. There were also two digest-sized items, enclosed in soft plastic bags covered with print. We'd no idea what those were, exactly, but I was eager to find out. They leaned against the fronts of blocking boards on the lowest of the two smutty rows.

The layout of the Bookstore was such that the cashier counter was elevated several feet from the rest of the sales floor. Long was this counter. Thick with stacks of discount items and a hodgepodge of promotional material.

Such configuration made the cash register a veritable crow's nest for whichever clerk was on duty. From their raised vantage, aided by a cleverly angled mirror in the shop corner, any cashier was able to see all the way down the magazine aisle.

Most vexingly, whoever manned the till had easy, direct sightline to the porno. The clerk would always be able to see us.

We'd have to go to tiptoes to even reach the goods.

The mags in bags would be noisy.

Nabbing those would have to be timed for when no other customer was present in the magazine aisle or another aisle adjacent.

Not to mention there was always the chance the shop's door could open without warning.

First thing some customer would see upon entry might easily be us, en flagrante.

What a mess to sort.

Alain was fit to be tied.

As far as he saw it, we'd have to wait for a lucky moment.

Grab.

Bolt.

He may've been right.

Regardless, as days passed it became clear he was eager and willing to resort to such common criminality. It didn't matter to him if we were caught.

But it mattered to me.

Not *being caught*, in principle.

But to be apprehended in such thoughtlessness?

I couldn't let my reputation be so pedestrian.

Added to which, why content ourselves with one clumsy lift?

A little attention to detail and we could graze from these racks as freely as we could the candy aisle at the Drugstore.

It was a matter of grasping the full picture.

Taking each portion in turn.

Defusing. Taming.

Our primary advantage was how there tended to only ever be one person manning the establishment. As they couldn't be expected to draw a paycheck for lounging in front all the doo-dah day, they were often lost amongst the aisles, tending to whichever menial tasks. Customers would ding a bell at checkout to summon them.

This lack of staff made it permissible for idlers like Alain and myself to sit around for as long as we pleased. We made cozy perch upon the piles of the remaindered books arranged at the opposite side of the magazine rack from our targets.

We'd be left undisturbed for however long.

Read kung-fu mags, movie mags, the comics we'd bought.

Munch on our stolen candy.

From so remote a spot, though, we'd never know exactly when the clerk stepped away from the front.

Not without a wander toward the mirrored corner for a peek.

Too many of those with the clerk still present would mark us something queer.

Plus, we got the hint how grown-up customers were shy to select the dirty magazines for legitimate purchase with us sat nearby. These patrons could be our friend's dads, our future school teachers, neighbors aspiring for local office. They'd mill around, leafing through whichever mags else, their annoyance at our loitering palpable.

One word from one of them to store staff and we might be told not to hang round, full stop.

Already we were pushing our luck by never spending a dime on premises. No percentage making ourselves sore thumbs with hours of fruitless recon.

What we needed was to make it seem like being in the Bookstore was only ever of peripheral interest to us.

If we stood outside the store, off a distance, the counter area was seventy-percent visible. We'd more-or-less know when we had a window of time to strike without ever having to go through the doors.

I came up with a schematic for us to put this power to the most streamlined use.

Every other day, we'd pop in when it seemed the front was unmanned.

If customers were present by the magazines, no opportunity presented to get at our prize, we'd exit straight away.

Since the clerk couldn't have clocked us, we'd go back to monitoring the window. Bonus, we'd know exactly how many people we had to wait to clear out while also able to keep track of whoever else went in.

If no customers were present but the clerk for some reason returned to the front, our posture would be how we were big fans of science-fiction and fantasy books, that genre being what lined the shelf against the shop's front wall which jointed to the porn corner. We'd waste a few minutes gabbing to each other how 'once we saved up' we'd buy this or that book.

Then we'd leave.

I did my best to make Alain cognizant how these hijinks were in service of seizing the day when a quick minute presented itself wherein the cashier counter was untended and no customer was at hand.

When such stars aligned, one of us would lean against the interior of the shop's door to ensure an unobtrusive spot of interference to any customer suddenly showing up. The pause caused in such eventuality should ensure enough time that the other of us could still make a beeline for the corner, grab down at least one mag, no matter what. Worst come of worse, the precaution would allow for the mission to abort without prejudice.

We'd not make off with whatever boodle was lifted from the rack, there-and-then. Rather, we'd stash the contraband under the discounted coffee-table books we sometimes sat on.

The tip was to dribble the goods systematically away from the corner.

Once we had one of every title placed elsewhere about the store we could arrange to collect.

Sometimes we'd each ferry out one mag at-a-time. Curling them around our shins. Elastic of socks keeping them fit to place.

Other times we'd load several onto our persons, at once. Front of pants. Back of pants. Around one shin. An issue each in our respective bags.

When we'd plan a bulk pick-up like that, we'd purchase a novel.

I quite enjoyed the brazen moment of hitting the summon bell. Interrupting the clerk's duties. Getting a prim 'Thank you' as we walked out.

Before unloading our steal to a single bag, Alain and I would need to cross the entire length of the Shopping Center.

We paraded by. A performance piece.

Two children. Each with one leg stiff. Peculiar suggestion of limp. Bodies held stiffly upright as though imitating effete upper-class twits from sketch comedy.

We nodded to folks enjoying ice creams on outdoor benches, barbers taking cigarette breaks.

Our awkwardness was calculated. Zany camouflage to ensure no accidental betrayal of secreted merchandise due to an odd drape of our clothing's baggy fabric.

How we were never waylaid, made to explain ourselves, baffles me.

Had adults no eyes in their skulls?

Or were we perhaps a pleasant sight?

A trigger. A prompt for some shared shiver of nostalgia throughout them.

These people keeping our secrets to better leave unperturbed their own.


GIDDY RODENTS, CHEEKS FULL, WE sniffed out a spot to bury our illicit acorns.

Twenty or so yards from the main road surrounding the housing development. The perma-moist grass beneath a patch of trees in rear of the neighborhood swimming pool. Underneath ample fallen pine needles, green, rust brown, rust orange, littered thick.

There was a scuzziness to this environment we'd instinctually ferreted as the best home for our sins.

Glanced in passing while driving by it left a sour impression. A divot like a scab always gluey.

Before long, our paranoia led us to shift ground.

Being sighted in transit to-or-from the spot might alert the nosey to nose.

Sagacity suggested our growing cache find new home to the side of our usual path in-and-across the main vein of the creek. Our venturing into and out from these woods would be expected. No eye would bat twice.

As protection against the elements, Alain brought some mega-sized Ziploc bags from home. We secured the sheathed nasties in hollows beneath logs. Tangles of prickers. Snuggled under ropes of sumac.

The season shifted winterward.

The trees securing sight of the creek's interior turned to skeleton fingers, no longer cover enough to hide us from possible curious glances out townhouse windows while we flipped pages. Shivered. Sniffled.

We sought out a final home for our stash near one of the large, concrete sewer tunnels, deep in the guts of the woods.

Despite being a stone's throw from the Child Care Center, this clubhouse was the most secure of all. Noises of play, jump-rope song, bratty whining, shrieks from skinned knees were soundtrack to our kinky perusals.

Sometimes we'd hang around in this nook even when not preening over our treasures. Chat. Relax. Together. Alone.

Invisible right at plain sight's periphery.

It became less than challenging to make each new boost of the smut.

An afterthought.

No more adrenalin to it than pocketing chewing gum.

Where there'd once been fascination now, again, there was only activity.

I think back the near thirty years to my shoulders cold and itching through my sweatshirt against that cement. Think of the intricacy of the thieving. The diligence of the collecting. The meticulousness of the concealment.

Weeks.

Months.

Twenty then forty then well past one-hundred magazines.

An era wherein my primary vocation seems it must've been the curation of this nudie Alexandria.

Yet I don't recall the endeavor being of primacy.

From that stretch of my childhood I truthfully recall more moments nothing at all to do with the images I saw in the stolen pages than I do those spent fixated on them.

To what end the effort, then?

One of the great mysteries to me is what on Earth I did with all that naughty stuff.

What purpose did it serve?

What real kick did it offer?

Other than the occasional, involuntary *sproing* of stiff attention, my sexuality hadn't reached crisis. No. The typical use for such stimuli was some time away.

As for Alain?

I've no idea how he utilized thoughts of the pornography in private. But during the hours we spent elbow-to-elbow, turning pages like morning papers in a drama of Thatcher's England, he made no tawdry display. Between us transpired no innocent 'Show me yours, I'll show you mine' such as people seem to expect there must've when I tell stories of these capers to workmates or at social functions.

The appearance of the men and the women in the photospreads bored me terrifically after the initial jolts and shivers.

They didn't look like people.

Like anyone of this world.

By which I don't mean they struck me heavenly, sublime, unattainably, indisputably attractive.

Quite the contrary.

The nudity seemed concocted. A false front.

Naked to be not.

Even in full wingspan of carnality, these bodies were less beguiling than dozens of people, fully clothed, going about life, who glimpses of would fascinate my not-yet-teenaged mind in the course of any given day.

Alain was the more typical lad, I suppose.

For him, breasts were the-falser-the-better. Buttocks ought fit cupped in the palm, the size and the pert of a Granny Smith apple. Any entwinement of two females constructed thus was one he vowed he'd sell his soul for proximity to.

Often, Alain would position his hands to block from view any penis which appeared in a photograph.

This confused me.

At the very least, the presence of those zap-guns gave some frame-of-reference to any goings on. Made what was depicted anatomically, physiologically, abstractly pertain to me.

Alain'd poke fun at certain male models not of as fit physique as others. He smelled a rat.

'They must pay to get in there.'

He'd suspect the same of women who in some bend might show contours and gravity more realistic.

I remember once saying to Alain 'Everyone is paid or they wouldn't be there.'

He looked at me with pity. The wariness in his features as he cocked his brow lingers even now before my eyes.

Alain, at twelve, possessed fervent desire that life could be fantasy.

I lamented, at eleven, how fantasy failed to be life.

Was less.

Designed painstakingly to not resemble it.

As concern for titillation diminished, its replacement became a fascination with learning the intricacies of the various titles' particular restrictions. Inspecting, cataloging the nitty-gritty of different volume's formatting.

Some magazines only had pin-up style spreads. Women depicted solo. Posed extravagant.

Other titles alternated scenes depicting woman alone, man-with-woman, woman-with-woman, man-with-woman-with-woman, so on.

I came to discern how in certain mags the minimal descriptive text accompanying spreads at least superficially tried to match up with a narrative suggested by the images versus others wherein generic, disembodied phrasings were utilized.

It got where I'd be able to guess correctly how many pages each type of scenario would go on for.

Which manner of activity would be depicted on each page in sequence.

The particular composition of the photos each fantasy would end on.

I only honestly enjoyed the portions of photospreads where the parties were clothed at least partially. Would follow the shedding of layers with keen attention.

Coat coming off.

Button-down unbuttoned.

Camisole and panties, now.

Now, only socks.

When nakedness showed full, a frame-of-reference jumped.

Context was lost.

Alain had favorite models.

I suppose I had, too.

But while his were based on generalized requirements like bust-size, mine were borne of what'd be seen as oddities, even flaws, to someone like him.

Features I might've seen elsewhere in life became exotic flourishes on the page.

This woman with red hair cropped short.

That with a face more handsome than feminine.

The bulbs of this one's shoulder were littered in freckles four colors.

That one had three asymmetric moles on her hip.

Photographs submitted by readers were the most potent intoxicants. I thought the figures in them singularly enchanting. Possessed of magic. Of genius. Of everything to commend. Weightless. Holy.

These women were pickpockets-in-reverse. Trying to slip beauty where beauty wasn't valued. Flesh, mind, and purpose snuck where there was otherwise only fantasia.

They looked like people one might meet.

Had met.

People who people might be.

Alain, of course, heaped contempt on these images. Couldn't find derision enough. They were so spare, the photographs. So poorly lit. Washed out. Acne plain. Desperate. These ladies didn't have what it took to be *models*.

'They're just *ugly*' he'd go so far as to sneer. A child with another in the woods with a stolen magazine.

I enjoyed tremendously the periodicals' dingy back pages. Black-and-white. Pulp stock paper even when the rest of the magazine was cheapo gloss. Dozens of capsule advertisements crammed onto each one.

I adored the newsprint ordinariness of the women depicted in the bulk of the Chat Line adverts. Daguerreotype, almost. Glammed up a bit, sure, but the way someone regular might try their hand at glamour.

I could see these people as lonely.

Think them appreciative of conversation. Ideas.

Genuinely wondering was anybody going to call.

Who?

Why?

Knowing who.

Knowing why.

Hoping not.

Not bothered if.

That I knew the photos were unconnected to any voice which might answer a call made me fall in love with the voices, unheard.

The letters from readers were my favorite. I cherished them. How they removed the need for someone else's images to clutter my mind. The men, the women in the confessions could be however I pleased. Even the extant descriptions didn't matter. Pointless coding. I'd no idea what it meant when a woman's measurements were jotted out like chess notation. Weight as digits or skin as color had no choice but to bend to my own poetics.

The urgency of any fantasy, the revelation of shared desire, seemed much more real when rendered in words. No matter if the letters related actual events as they postured.

Fantasies were as much actual event as actual events ever were fantasy.

Secrets.

Whether truth or fantasy. These letters were secrets.

Shared with thieves. Or with thieves most honestly.

Thieves who'd not ask if the truth was a fantasy.

Who didn't care.

Thieves only wanted the secrets.

Stole them only to keep.

THE HUMDRUM OF A SUMMER'S typical day. The rote motions of standard fare lift. Alain and I.
Except not so.
I could tell. Yet I couldn't.
Laden down with oatmeal cookies, I was ready to exit the Drugstore. Alain, however, seemed antsy. He eyeballed the checkout area. Face at calculated squint. His speech and movements robotic when I inquired was anything the matter.
He wasn't ready to go?
No.
Did he think we'd been made, should ditch our haul?
No.
The clerk up front, was he worry they'd accost us?
No.
I finally got from him how he needed to steal something they only kept near the registers. He remained evasive as to what.
My own inspection of the checkout gave no clue.
Nothing there we couldn't nab elsewhere.
One of the cold sodas in the cooler?
I'd buy it for him if he was broke.
No no no. He told me to just head home without him. He'd see me later on.
On the walk back to the neighborhood I came under a spiteful cloud. The sunlight centered in a sweat-bead headache exactly above the crinkle-scarred bridge of my nose.
That'd been a heavy-duty brush off I'd in no way deserved.
What'd he said exactly?
'Nothing *you* would need.'
'Nothing *you* know about.'
So there went our in-it-together.
My counsel, strategy not sought.
Rankled, I moped about my living room.
What could be at the bottom of this?

Best I reckoned was he'd simply wanted me gone. Maybe he was meeting someone else. The brusque air to shoo me.

I poured over recent interactions for indication my company had worn out its welcome.

So far as I was concerned, he was free to go his own way. Yes, it stung to think he felt it beneath him to put things to my face, but I didn't want to get beside myself.

We'd been friends for a year-and-change. Had a history.

He might be in a transitional place, of course. Uncertain how best to comport himself. Might feel awkward broaching a perceived fissure.

Lord knew I'd known such teeter-totting. Even with regard to him, were I honest.

However, I could only be so magnanimous.

If some third-party were involved it concerned me directly. Whoever the newcomer was got keys to the kingdom I'd had hand in building.

It was one thing for Alain to cut me out of his life, but a horse of an altogether different color to bring someone else in.

Give an outsider access to our hideout.

Allow them a share in the spoils of methods I'd originated.

What would Alain play at?

Credit himself for everything?

Efface me?

Or was he now in cahoots with the sort of brigand who'd think it spectacular I was being backstabbed?

Would a mockery of me be part of their bond?

Enough was enough.

My head was no country to dwell in.

I'd need to check it out.

Alain feeling petulant didn't give him sovereignty. I had every right to show up to the clubhouse whenever I pleased. If he acted put off by my arrival, I'd know all.

I didn't need him any more than he needed me, if one were to be scientific about it.

He could have the sewer.

I might even let him have the library, too.

I left my house.

Made for the woods.

My progress through the underbrush was cautious. Careful to keep my breathing measured. Disperse the crunch of gravel, pebble, silt, the water trickle, the burps of my footfalls on the slippery clay outskirts of the creek-bed where I had to hug close to steep upcroppings of earth to traverse.

When I first sighted Alain it was with a jazz of relief I'll never forget.

There he was.

Lounged back like always.

Knees slightly bent to support a mag gingerly flopped open.

I recall the exact change in my chest the next blink.

The rotting of a bulbous guffaw I'd breathed in to make ready.

The clamping down of the 'Hey, man' I'd intended to *Boo* in jocular surprise.

Alain brought a cigarette to his mouth.

Sun through the tree branches inked him in a patchwork of misshapen shadow while he took a drag.

Lowered his arm.

Flipped a page.

I watched him let out a thin grey exhalation. The slow, even line of it taut like piano wire.

I froze.

Terrified he'd look up.

Slasher film scenario. I'd seen too much. Had wandered where I oughtn't have. Was intruder. My coming butchery my own fault for wondering what was behind that metal door by the stairs where Leatherface lived.

The backpedaling, the scurrying home is a memory one-second long and ten-thousand years. Both version featureless.

However it happened, next thing I knew I was in my living room, hissing to myself 'I mean, what do I care?'

I postured a bit how this development was unfathomable.

Only some few weeks prior, in conversation with an adult neighbor, we'd both ridiculed the sort of dolts who'd start smoking when they knew the risks. Promised we'd never undertake something so without reward.

So he'd lied.

What was he supposed to've said?

Same as I'd say if the conversation had been about stealing pornography, no doubt. Had that with-adult conversation been about thieving, we'd have put on pious hats but then joined in privately mocking the dotard, diminishing their lowliness for clinging to norms.

We'd think them gutless.

Not explorers like us.

But to deceive me?

Keep this theft and this act his own?

What did Alain make of me?

Some hump?

Beneath him?

This was his declaration we were not of a cloth.

Which perhaps we weren't.

But for him to declare himself the finer silk, the soul possessed of the holier secret?

Damn him to Hell, there.

I paced from sulks on the sofa to peeks out the front window curtains.

Before long, I saw Alain appear at the head of the field, under the power-lines. Saw him continue toward the back of my house.

So moved to the living room window.

Watched him pass under the tree branches. Amble down the way. Toward the park. To the rear of the neighborhood with his own back door.

That's how it was, then.

I spent perhaps ten minutes oscillating between writing him allowances and cursing his offspring for generations hence.

Then left out my door.

I have little pristine memory of my next actions. Even here as I recall the deeds, mostly it's recollecting a sensation of tightness. Of ticking clock. Of shaking. Of fear.

I wrested the bagged magazines from their hibernation.

Tugged bunches out of plastic bags at-a-time.

I tore covers.

Shredded pages.

Crumpled them.

Stamped down and screwed my foot side-to-side, fanning entire issues to smithereens.

I hurled waste after waste down into the bag-brown water where if a leg sunk in it'd be to the ankle.

Finally, huffing, indiscriminate, I chucked entire, untorn volumes into the soup.

Armfuls. Underhand. Forklift.

With zeal I panted and growled until the entire amount of our ill-gotten take was soaking bloated in the stream.

Clotting the water.

Pages fusing in a smear of pulpy cartilage there'd be no rescuing a single image from.

If I was no longer to be had, no longer was any of this.

If the piece of me Alain had torn away and discarded was of no value to him, then these pieces come of me which he so treasured were lost to him, too.

Back home.

I recall the density of the shaded living room. Can almost hear how a tuning fork would whine in matching the tone it'd took. The slant of light through the windows was aggressively angular. Thick. Sharp. Like stale peanut brittle.

The horror of my act. The finality.

There was no returning from it.

The corpses would be found, no fooling.

Before the sun was down.

How would I defend myself?

Defend?

I'd nothing to defend. I'd fulfilled a circuit Alain had begun. He was responsible. I was the outcome of his mechanism. I refused to let the consequence be assigned to me when I'd done nothing to perturb the tranquility which'd birthed and preserved what'd just been destroyed.

*Bang-bang-bang* came the knocks.

In a state of unearthly calm I turned the knob. Opened the door with a smiled 'Hey, man.'

Alain was a discombobulated mound of inarticulateness.

I needed to come. To come now. Something had happened. He couldn't even think how to explain.

His face. The most ignorant one I'd ever seen. The most commonplace. His face was the perfect configuration for the mind within it. The consciousness which couldn't fathom this situation. His wretched face lacked the breeding to comprehend.

The dullard kept gawping and stammering half-explanations as he hurried me along. Kept spouting how he didn't understand.

Kept asking 'Who would do this?'

Soon we were stood above the aftermath.

I made all the requisite postures. The Oh-my-Gods. Gaped down. Acted awestruck by the sight of this Antietam Creek of smut. Alain idiotically tried to fish out some survivors.

The weakling pages, sopping wet, mixed with each other, tore at his slightest touch.

After twenty minutes, he'd managed a pathetic little collection of body parts.

Spread the pages out to dry.

Hoping the sultry air would stiffen them.

The sun's rays would cure them of their leprosy.

We sat and fumbled at theories, together.

The poor little fool.

Come on, Alain.

You're smart enough to know it was me, aren't you?

Light your precious cigarette.

Jab it at me j'accuse.

Stub it in my traitorous eye.

But Alain was a person like a shirtsleeve. Limp and store bought.

An accusation cost more than he was.

I sometimes think he knew he'd no recourse to vengeance.

What could he take from me considering what he'd taken, already?

Maybe he knew he was left what he was without me.

That I was what I was without him.

Either way, we were done.

He'd simply never say it.

As we walked back toward the neighborhood, I shrugged and tried to chuff him up.

Did he want to hang out?

Our favorite cartoon should be just about on.

No.

He should go home. He needed to think.

'Well, good luck with that' I almost said.

Said instead, after a nod, 'It's too bad. But everything's fine.'

.part two.

.1.

MIDDLE-SCHOOL WAS A KIND of hothouse hybrid of Victorian steam kitchen and Soviet gulag. All the charm of lanced buboes.

Or at least so I gleaned from what little time I'd spend there.

Anything I could do to wriggle free of the place became my passion, very quickly.

Even before arrival, day one, the die was cast.

Alain didn't venture near me at the bus stop in the morning. When, en route to school, I summoned nerve to make my way back to where he was sitting my gaffe was visibly clear.

We'd not spoken in weeks, but his wordless dismissal was unnerving.

Addled with disquiet, I made a second attempt. Prepared to whisper some bizarre nonsense concerning how I'd stumbled on information revealing who'd destroyed our magazines.

Got so far as intoning, conspiratorial, that I had something I needed to tell him before he curtly stated 'Tell me later.'

All four syllables fanged.

His eyes moving from mine signified our interactions being permanently shuttered.

It struck me Alain was the only soul I'd know among the multi-thousand soon to surround me.

Fine. I'd start with blank slate. Head down.

It was just school.

Except it turned out I was an immediate pariah.

No matter that most students were utter strangers to each other, I was marked the lowest caste on sight.

Before, even.

An aura preceding me.

Anyone I saw could walk up to anyone else, perform a greeting of whichever custom, and at the very least be interacted with cordially.

Contrawise, my approach was immediately awarded side-eyes or worse, even if I was simply asking where a classroom was.

There seemed no excuse for my thinking a 'Hello' to one of my peers would be returned nor for my seeming belief there existed apologies enough for the bother it'd caused whomsoever.

Those who came up to me did so for purposes of subversive ridicule I'd fail to grasp the satire in.

A kid made a point to tell me he liked my *Miss Saigon* shirt.

'Nice one' I thought. Seemed innocent enough.

But no sooner did I smile, fumbling to come up with a way to capitalize on my good fortune, than the speaker's back turned. In-the-know chortles bubbling from all classroom corners.

I'd be approached at random with demands to have the most far-fetched and scurrilous rumors confirmed or denied.

Had I eaten a spider outside of Shop class?

Was it true I'd had to go home for soiling myself twice in one day in fourth-grade?

That was me, right?

I had a medical condition?

An encounter which rattled me fundamentally was when a group of girls told me they'd heard I was banned from the mall for stealing pantyhose eggs from *JC Penny*.

Was it a fact I'd cried to get out of my mom being called?

I was surrounded.

Stammered an admission that I certainly *would* steal pantyhose eggs. Had often *thought* about it. But never *had*.

'I've never been *caught* stealing in my life' I emphasized. 'But I steal things, sure.'

I'd try to remind myself the words 'No comment' existed in English.

But somehow the words and their spirit seemed the worst tack I might take. I could feel my negative reputation budding like overzealous yeast anytime I'd take the approach of walking away.

I'd not come off stoic, Zen, imperturbable.

Just a standoffish bedbug.

My psyche capsized under these public assails.

When on their heels came shoves and insinuations of deviant sexuality I was too numb to much care.

It didn't seem to me Alain had caused this generalized vendetta. Maybe he'd struck an initial flint, but the reality in play was beyond his powers by orders of magnitude.

No doubt the group he'd fallen in with talked ill of me amongst themselves. But they seemed to have no specific campaign against me.

Besides which, Alain was no leader.

A flunky, at best.

A hanger-on in a group with only subpar popularity overall.

I attempted leaning into the swirling rumors and whichever jibe, hoping this might diffuse them.

'Circling back to clarify, girls: yes, I ate that bug. I was merely confused when you'd asked me, before. It wasn't a spider. It was the fly in the spider's web. Looked so plump and delicious, who would blame me? Pardon the crossed wires.'

'Why am I wearing a *Miss Saigon* shirt? What's it supposed to mean? I see your point, sir. I wouldn't wear it myself, except for an ironic sense of pride. It's all on account of I won a contest. A little bit of music I composed was worked into one of the show's big numbers. You know the bit where the helicopter lands? The tune right before that is a variation on something I submitted to a youth Arts magazine. You must understand, it's this anecdotal history which compels me to keep the garment in circulation, nothing more.'

I took to entering every class late so I'd not have to mingle while things settled down. Would have reason to be in conference with the teacher while everyone else filed out at the bell.

When this failed, I took to hiding in the bathroom.

Once I was pegged a lavatory loiterer, I tried spinning the medical condition rumors to some advantage.

Vicious dyspepsia.

Chronic.

Hereditary.

But this backfired exactly how I ought to've expected.

Obviously my explanation was dubbed a lie.

Word got round that what I was, in fact, was a habitual masturbator who produced reproductive fluid in incomprehensible amounts.

A White-Out splotch on my backpack was evidence of as much.

That's what I employed to cover up my spills.

I was clever enough not to volunteer the information that I'd never yet ejaculated.

Probably this tacitness saved me from a literal gallows being erected.

Any method of reimagining myself or presenting a new iteration brought worse result.

Even going the legitimate route, selling out.

I tried to join afterschool Drama Club.

For no discernable reason, flat off the mark, the way I'd perform any scene was met with aghast reaction from those with clout. I was either taking things way too far, behaving like a half-wit, or needed to be reminded I was supposed to be acting.

'Acting, you know? Have you ever even heard of it?'

Due to the fantastic luck of having a mom who was worked like a dog, day shifts and overnights, it was fairly easy to arrange to cut school. Even occasions where my mom was around in the mornings, my dad being a medical man allowed him final say regarding whether I was to stay home or not.

Even better luck, he didn't seem much bothered with catching me out in a fast one.

My personality profile of the old man was instrumental in making my scheme take. Many were the ways it could've gone wrong had someone slightly more sensible or suspicious been my adversary.

No doubt I'd have worked something out, regardless.

Still, it was fun to concoct plans which not only worked but proved me keenly insightful regarding the predictability of individual behaviors.

I developed a precise method for manipulating the glass, mercury based thermometer, for example.

Would have a lightbulb prepped hot before the thing was given me.

Knowing my dad would be lost in his work papers while having me sit on the sofa a full five minutes with the contraption under my tongue made it easy to work out an exact timing for getting covertly to the lit bulb.

Thermometer held to it the count of five.

Glass given delicate shakes enough to bring the liquid silver down to the temperature-line equated with just-feverish-enough.

In the odd duck occurrence where he'd have me sit in the same room as him, I'd shift to subtler means.

I knew from observation that 'no fever' didn't necessarily queer the deal.

I'd perform the song-and-dance of describing a vague constellation of symptoms which I knew he felt it was bad medicine to ignore.

Endless riffs on sore throat, headache, tummy ache, lethargy, nausea.

Often quite captivating and poetic.

Never came off like I was quoting a medical text.

Only trying to present the most accurate picture I could.

The more intricate, personalized the detail, the more ways his mind would abstract something out, find legitimate cause for concern.

There were mornings where, out of the blue, he'd insist I attend classes even if we'd agreed otherwise the night previous.

On these days I was well aware I could wait him out.

If I kept to the bathroom, he'd eventually get bored.

Cut his losses.

Drive off to his much more pressing business of mathematical research at the *National Institute of Health*.

I became a dab hand at forging the old man's fairly incomprehensible signature. Even got good enough at counterfeiting the boilerplate remarks he'd jot on excuse notes that I didn't have to trace them.

Oftentimes, I'd not even bother presenting notes.

The teachers would simply look at me befuddled when I'd arrive, assuming I'd checked in with the Front Office as I ought to've.

If I went to the Front Office window without a note, I'd say I forgot it.

Suggest they try calling my dad.

I doubt they much bothered.

The only drag was I literally couldn't swallow capsules.

Never had been able to.

Not the tiniest tablet.

Due to this handicap, I had to develop a rarified set of skills for palming, cheeking, otherwise faking that ibuprofen or whatever had been ingested.

I'd rather have swallowed the unnecessary meds, truth be told.

My entire subterfuge would blow up in my face over a single slip-up.

I went so far as trying to put the various caplets inside pieces of bread or doughnut to down them proper.

But on two consecutive occasion I'd been unable to chew around them enough to work a swallow.

Crunched down on the pills hard.

The deplorable taste in my mouth put me off this approach forever.

It was a lot of work just to be no place.

But worth it.

As that was the one place I wanted to be.

INCENTIVE FOR GOING TO SCHOOL was cash. Not on purpose. But cash.

My dad was in charge of lunches.

The practice of leaving brown bags with flimsy peanut-butter sandwiches and baggies of peanuts inside had been retired.

Each morning, now, there was a loose leaf of paper waiting on the dining table.

My name written, top left.

Older brother's name at top right.

Paper-clipped to this would be two five-dollar bills.

A week of school guaranteed me twenty-five clams.

One month yielded one-hundred.

This was insane in some respects.

It was those respects I respected.

If I didn't go to school a certain day, I'd not have cash to pocket.

Though if I orchestrated my skip, last minute, the money was usually already laid out.

Not supposed to take it, but I would.

Often, the next morning there'd be money, again.

My dad, thus, was a very lovable man.

I seldom ate.

Never at school.

No reason to spend the money on snacks down at the Shopping Center.

Though sometimes I would.

Just because.

Subsidized thus, thievery a vocation rather than a middle-finger to socioeconomic status or the powers-that-be, one might think I'd have had zero appetite to bite the hand which fed me.

In truth, I don't recall there existing such impulse.

Nonetheless, I made it my business to grift from my dad's wallet with increasing regularity.

Of great curiosity to me, age forty looking back at age twelve, is how it could have been that so far along into a life spent cogitating on theft I'd still not developed a sensitive understanding of money.

An innate, anti-capitalistic sentiment?

I suspect mere aloofness. Some asbestos lining muffling my willingness to make *sound* decisions over *interesting* ones.

I'd develop plans.

Keep painstaking in my methods.

Such plans and pains continually evidenced as unnecessary.

It was the stupefying way the stealing kept working which drew me to pickpocket my dad, again and again.

That plus the comfort of having a fix for my addiction right at home, what else could I have done?

In the same hall closet where during my criminal infancy I'd taken so much joy stashing my mom's twenty-dollar bill, my dad hung his heavy old coat. So well I recollect the visible weight of its beige. The always-cold feel of its outer sleeves.

In the left-side pocket, amongst wadded, used tissues and tissues wadded, unused, the bulky leather billfold would be.

There'd typically be money.

Plenty.

Or plenty-from-a-child's-point-of-view, anyway.

But I'd never count how much.

Never.

No matter how I scour my memory-banks for a solitary instance of 'Dad has $X$ dollars' the variable is ever unresolved.

I'd survey the bills present of a given snatch with meticulousness.

Four *twenties*. Three *tens*. Seven *fives*. Eleven *ones*.

But never once did I do the sums to achieve the total amount I'd be subtracting from.

*One-hundred seventy-six dollars.*

Nor would I ever tabulate the amount I'd take.

*Sixteen dollars.*

I'd think of it as one *ten*, one *five*, one *one*.

Since the difference in each individual $X$ was negligible, I concluded the difference would pass unremarked.

$X$, be it *twenties*, *tens*, *fives*, had been *six* and now $X$ was *five*.

My pop'd simply assume he was 'off by one'.

Reckon he must've misremembered which $X$ was which.

How many of each $X$ he'd had.

Sheer lunacy.

Looking back I know my dad hadn't concluded 'I thought I had *two* twenties, now I only have *one*. But *one* is only *one-less* than *two*, so whatcha gonna do?'

He'd know he'd had *forty* dollars.

*Twenty* dollars of which was gone.

Know there'd been *one-seventy-six*.

Now there was *one-sixty*.

He was a mathematical researcher.

A former medical doctor.

Had been awarded multiple PhDs.

Had these thoughts occurred to me, real time, I'd have barreled ahead all the same.

I loved my tabulations.

Besides which, if he caught me he caught me.

Business as usual.

The takes from the wallet were semi-regular at first. I'd go that route only when I'd missed several days of school and lunch money hadn't been left out.

Hardly stealing. The cash'd been earmarked.

Mine in spirit.

*Semi-regular* became *more-semi-regular*.

Became *regular*.

Such an easy groove to get fit to.

I should've been caught but hadn't been.

As always, this made the experience serene. A soak in bubbled bathwater.

Some decisions which in retrospect beggar belief crossed my mind those days, too.

I'd make steals while my dad was in the next room.

On purpose.

Task myself with learning to creep down from upstairs in perfect silence.

Get the closet open.

Slip hand soundlessly into coat pocket.

Wallet brought out.

Its load lightened.

All while the man I was bilking could stand up any moment, with one step have me red-handed.

My view was that enacting the steals while he was near-at-hand, but enacting them in such method which gave the illusion I'd been upstairs at the time of the theft, awarded me plausible deniability.

Despite he'd neither know when the thefts took place nor where I'd been.

Again: sheer lunacy.

But, again: the evidence of my success gave me no call to question.

When it came to pass that the wallet stopped being in the coat pocket, I concluded the jig was up.

Except I'd not been given a talking to.

There was still lunch money left, every day.

Other than the fact the wallet well had run dry, life went on remarkably uninterrupted.

By chance, I discovered my dad had taken to keeping his wallet inside his briefcase.

His briefcase with a combination lock.

Pretty smart.

Equally smart, he actually scrambled the code-dial when he secured the metal, alligator-toothed latches.

But how much did he scramble it?

I made surreptitious observations. Ascertained that it took some effort to rotate the three numerals for each latch.

Further reconnaissance illustrated that when my dad closed the briefcase he did nothing more than wriggle his thumb pads on the combination dials.

Not even one second spent.

Sometimes he didn't even do that.

So perhaps the numbers I'd see on display, any given time, were only a tap off, higher-or-lower, than the numbers which would grant access.

If this were so, there were only some few permutations I'd have to investigate.

Sure, I could've waited out an opportunity to snap a quick glimpse at the dials when the briefcase was open. Or else could've bided my time, jumped at the chance for a gander after he'd closed it on one of the occasions he'd neglected to manipulate the lock.

But I made it a point-of-pride to figure out the puzzle without cribbing off the answer-key.

That wouldn't be fun.

I liked fun.

My third guess was the correct combination.

So every few nights I'd remain awake until the wee hours.

Sneak my way down to the dining room.

Quiet as a flea, I'd open the case.

Relieve the wallet of some funds.

Close the case.

Reset the lock to exactly what it'd displayed before my ministrations.

I recall being quite put out on occasions there weren't enough of each denomination to allow for pocketing anything.

A few times the wallet was entirely devoid of cash and I'd snarled.

Not out of greed.

Rather, for the wasted effort.

I was depriving myself of sleep, risking capture each time out.

At least a buck should come of that.

Soon the wallet wasn't in the briefcase or the coat pocket.

It wasn't anyplace.

Worse. It was someplace. Just someplace I'd no clue how to discover. Was no place *reasonable*.

My initial consideration was my dad now kept it in his car. The glovebox.

I never checked, but grew to doubt this hypothesis.

He was too absentminded.

Would forget it all day long, that way.

Besides, hadn't I regularly seen him needing to go into the thing for certain cards with telephone numbers on them?

Was I to believe he'd suddenly recopied all that scratch-scratch into a notebook?

Such cumbersome precautions undertaken, steps entirely out of sync with his nature?

He'd changed fundamentally to miserly defend his fortune rather than saying 'Stop stealing from me, you cockroaches' to his children?

Hardly.

I made exactly one further guess about where the wallet might be. One hyper-specific, completely out-of-the-ether stab at it.

When it turned out correct, I felt I was a preternatural mentalist who ought be on salary for a world leader.

My dad's bathroom area was a nook attached to the master bedroom. A kind of *L* shaped cubby which stood always mildly humid. Scented minty and spiced from amounts of toothpaste and shaving foam collected in hardened lumps on the porcelain of the sink counter.

In this cloister was a closet.

In this closet hung shirts and sundries I don't believe the man ever wore.

Beneath these stood a long bureau. Three drawers high. Five normal drawers plus one longer drawer wide.

In the topmost right drawer, stuffed all the way back behind socks, each pair rolled into tight balls, was the wallet.

Was very purposefully *hidden* the wallet.

Upon discovery, I was too dumbfounded to take anything from it.

It didn't seem right.

Not then.

My dad being all the way downstairs made things too easy.

As much as I'd earned my payday and was awed by my extra-sensory criminality, I let be.

Come nightfall would be another story.

When my dad lay in bed snoring.

When I'd have to crawl into the room.

Pass him by.

Risk being cornered if he suddenly needed to relieve himself.

Such thieveries felt like being in love with something which loved me back in exact reciprocal.

The anxiety of the actions, the lack of consequence, made me feel unknown and understood.

SHAMBLING SHAMBLING SHAMBLING, I schlepped my thieving rounds at the Shopping Center. An undead. The most animation left to the corpse certain electrical pops in the forebrain. Pops producing ridiculous over-complications in methods for worming out of being apprehended.

I wanted to be caught.

Not for some Everyman reason.

I wasn't issuing a plea for help. Squirming, lashing to beacon my lonely humanity.

No.

I pointedly wanted to throw whoever might catch me into a mishmash of sophistry and chop logic that'd suffocate them.

Make it so they'd have to let me go.

Unable to say they'd *caught* me.

*Helped* me.

*Changed* me.

*Anythinged* me.

A zombie's daydream, I laced the aisles of the Art Supply Store. Anything and everything mine for the plucking.

But so what?

I wanted nothing. Even things I might say I wanted I knew were wanted for so impermanent a duration the want was nullified.

No time to *want* before *had* before *used* or *discarded*.

To lift this or that trinket was analogous to feeding a body riddled with tapeworm. No vital nourishment would trickle to me. Even if I glutted myself, all spoils would route to the parasites.

To the last crumb.

Bypassing natural avenues, my mind would chug and chug and chug, creating amok science. I'd come up with a way to keep myself fed intravenously.

It was now a cinch I'd always have enough money on me to purchase whichever item I might theoretically be caught trying to lift.

No need for cleverness.

The notion was I'd put items in a tote bag I'd carry. Not so overtly I'd be straightaway seen, but casually enough I was in no way avoiding notice.

If a representative of the store got huffy with me, I'd flash them a look suggesting they were behaving as though a madman.

Put on some vague accent of foreigner.

Speak in English theatrically broken yet easily understandable. I'd be so sorry.

'Of course I'd intended to pay. In my country, the custom is to collect the goods we wish to purchase and then bring our bagfuls to the cashier. All a cultural miscue. Please, explain to me what I ought do in future while I cheerily walk with you to pay for these items, presently.'

Such a drag I was never able to put this cartoon caper to the true test.

Shamble shamble shamble.

One time, I got the feeling I'd been clocked by a portly sales attendant.

I'd nothing on me yet, so was duly affronted by such attention.

Some customer service, eh?

Made me want to rob the place blind on principle.

If they were gonna peg me without cause they deserved whatever uppance came.

The injustice of the suspicion, considering how much most any other time it would've been perfectly just, only served to tick me off.

I had a field-day making this ham-hocked flatfoot get his exercise once I'd satisfied myself he'd no idea I was onto him.

Since he wasn't obliged to even approach me with an 'Anything I can help you find?' I felt more than obligated to waste an hour of his time.

He latched onto me, boffo go-getter, but kept a good distance remote.

If he was so worried about me stealing, why wasn't he acting to deter?

Seemed *Detective Colombo* wanted me to strike so he could be dubbed the hero.

Was this his warped notion of ethics?

I wandered into areas of the store which never interested me a jot.

Examined different types of yarn.

Picture frames.

Equipment to add beads to denim garments.

Hodgepodge of fake tree branches thick with false scented berries.

Faux-flowers meant to be assembled in squat vases.

Ghastly do-it-yourself potpourri.

I learned a great deal about what grown-ups got their sad enjoyments with. Enough recreation time spent in such bonkers pursuits to justify the existence not only of this store but its national and international franchise branches.

If I weren't but a husk, a decomposing tourist, such insights into members of the community where I dwelt might've given me the creeps.

Having had my fill of this gumshoe dogging me, I lingered near the sketchbooks.

Made dandy show of seeming unscrupulous.

Yessir, the store dick had the hots for me, now. I could tell it in a reflection he didn't know gave me sightline of him.

Nothing on my person still, I moved to the rearmost aisle of the establishment.

Canvases. Decorative, mass-produced art in ceiling-high displays.

Strolled toward the shop corner with exaggerated leisure.

Stiff postured.

*Portrait of a Lowlife*.

I'd turn my head enough to glean peripheral impression that *Inspector Javert* floated in wait at the other end of each aisle as I passed.

Five aisles left. Briefly concealed behind an endcap, knowing my pursuer would have his view obscured by endcap at the aisle's other side, I abruptly sprinted ahead half-dozen gargantuan strides.

Could hear the *clatter-clatter* of confused footfalls.

The *squeak* of heels on the polished store tile.

When it was certain *Kojak* was in the aisle past where I'd paused, I began moseying back in the direction I'd come.

Here he was.

Yes? Could I help him?

Why did I need to come with him, exactly?

Knew I'd taken ... what?

This man hated me. I could tell it. Down to his dandruff he despised me. Loathed me for how I purposefully patted myself all over, lifted my shirt to flash skin-and-bones belly. Taking it too far on purpose to flaunt I'd made him a monkey.

Got his goat good.

I was ordered to stay right where I was.

Better yet, he marched me to each aisle I'd passed since the sketchbook section.

Told me 'Halt' at the mouth of every one.

Proceeded to make a forensic sweep of the shelves.

The spaces beneath the shelves.

Leafed through every item on the endcap pegs.

Dug through the bins.

A miraculous show. I couldn't get enough. Stood speechless. Enthralled.

He thought I'd made a clever stash of the purloined item.

What superpower did this lunkhead think I possessed with which I could've gotten to any of the areas he was searching in order to have discarded a sketchbook?

In the brief flickers of time where I'd been out of his sight?

His fervor in proving his suspicions correct overran his rationality.

Even if he found something out-of-place, how in the name of Christ-our-father would he contend it had anything to do with me?

I almost wanted him to discover some suspicious merchandise behind the tight-fit boxes on a shelf he'd needed a ladder to get to.

When he came up dunce, as final resort he told me he didn't want to see my face in the store ever again.

Even a specimen of the reheated dead like me had to smile at that. I recall the sound of my breath and heartbeat while I drank in the glorious ways I could play the moment.

Put it right in his face that I'd be back the next day and the next and the next unless he could produce one iota of justification which suggested legally or per Store Policy I not be permitted?

Tell him 'Fine, but just let me buy this sketchbook I came in for, okay?' before proceeding to buy the exact one I knew he'd suspected me of having made a go at swiping?

But profound boredom hit me.

Pity, too. Vast pity.

This poor, poor man.

What road had led to him being him and to him being here with me?

'No problem. You don't have what I want, anyway' I finally quipped before slouching off.

Shambling shambling shambling my dead body went. My impulse to juke the system its only engine.

Even for no profit.

Especially for no profit.

Decidedly and specifically for no profit.

At my own expense, in fact.

Such fun.

I revisited my science-fiction, fantasy novel loving persona from the Bookstore theft days. Only this time I presented as a genuine paying customer.

Five days in-a-row I'd come in.

First day, I'd buy something. Make great gab with the cashier while the transaction rang.

Second day, I'd buy nothing, but still shoot the breeze.

Third day, another purchase with banter.

Fourth day, bought nothing. Told the cashier a joke I claimed I'd just learnt.

Fifth day, purchased nothing. Left with a novel secured in my coat pocket.

Half-a-week after, I came back with the stolen novel in a bag. Laid down a rap about how I'd grabbed the wrong book in a series. Oh gosh, it'd been so confusing when I'd started reading. Thankfully, I'd caught the mistake before long.

Could I swap it out?

Of course.

Alack, the proper book in the series wasn't there.

Such being the case, could I get my money refunded?

No, unfortunately I don't seem to have the receipt.

Store Credit?

Is that the best he could do for me?

'I'm in here all the time. I can check at home for the receipt, later. It must be somewhere. I was surprised it wasn't in the bag.'

Was he sure he'd handed me a receipt?

Didn't matter, he supposed.

Here was the cash back.

Shamble shamble shamble.

I tallied things up while I wandered the Electronics Store.

I'd bought two books.

Stolen one.

So that's three books.

Had returned the one, so that's two.

Was refunded the price of the third.

So that's me down the cost of one book.

But them down the conceit of their security.

With a little effort, I could've played with price-points. Bought two books. Stolen a third equal to the value of the first two, combined.

But two-for-the-price-of-one satisfied me.

More than enough

Because they'd not see it that way.

Not that they had it in them to see.

Shambling shambling shambling, I coursed the veins where once I'd lived.

IN THE PERFECT PLACE FOR it, I discovered the thing everybody wanted least in the world. The thing nobody anywhere was looking for. The thing I needed.

Rear corner of the Comic Shop.

Very last box in the row on the floor.

One of three containing miscellaneous back-issues not arranged by title or category.

Amidst a slush of items which existed only technically, the *Jademan Kung-Fu Special* fluxed at the verge of corporeality.

I don't think any other customer who frequented the store bought Jademan titles. I'd started, myself, through random chance. *Oriental Heroes* number twenty-five. Became a casual collector of the series. From it branched to *Drunken Fist*. Bought a good run of *The Force of Buddha's Palm*. Had given *Blood Sword* a fair shake. Even tried *Blood Sword Dynasty*. *Iron Marshall*.

If there were other customers who'd buy the odd title, none of them treated the volumes like I did. I'd examine the Credits page, every issue. The letter column. I'd read the copy of every advertisement every time I re-read an issue.

Which is where I'd first seen the *Kung-Fu Special* listed.

If some other reader had seen the same advert, they'd not noticed it.

If they'd noticed it, they didn't remember it.

It hadn't lived on.

A presence in their mind.

A reasonless entity.

A desire.

The *Kung-Fu Special* was nothing more than a promotional offering. Brief, standalone teaser stories from each of the company's offerings.

A meaningless trifle.

A Platonic ideal.

I'd never seen it on the New Release shelf. I'd certainly have bought it if I had.

Original price was buck-fifty.

Here in the bin it was stickered seven.

There was no question I could afford it.

But I didn't want to *afford* it.

I *wanted* it.

Only one obstacle stood in the way of my taking the beauty.

My rules.

Because while there were very few rules, there were rules, nonetheless.

This place. The Comic Shop. A sanctum.

The proprietors. My friends.

I understood the world's rules.

I understood my own rules.

The world's rules were right. I didn't contend otherwise.

My rules were right. Absolutely.

But *I* was wrong. Was always wrong. Had always been wrong. Always would be wrong. Ask anyone who knew me. If you could find someone. Ask anyone who didn't know me. They'd tell you.

Had I happened across this jewel at some no name shop located some no place town there'd be no qualm about the shoplift. In any other environment it'd make no sense not to take it.

But here?

Here it made sense not to. Yes.

But to me it made ten-thousand times sense how this was, in fact, the place from which it could be *most* taken.

Therefore, it made *less* sense than anyplace not to take it.

For a week I jousted inside myself.

Why not buy it?

My money wasn't my money. Just money I had.

But shouldn't such money be the last money used to purchase something truly desired?

Didn't doing that, irrefutably, mean I'd accepted the normal parameters of the world?

*Stolen* money to buy things I wanted to *steal*?

Was that different than *earning* money to buy things I'd then say I'd *earned*?

Would I be kowtowing to terms of value, how value was valued, terms set in some abstract stone nothing to do with individual desire or truth?

I didn't want to *steal* this thing.

Didn't want to *earn* it.

I wanted it to *be mine*.

The universe was known for playing pranks. Maybe the comic would be gone when I went back for it. Perhaps my noticing it had started an inexorable process which'd led some oddjob collector to it. There was every chance, through cosmic coincidence, I'd noticed it mere days before the Comic Shop was due to conduct inventory. A purge of flabby, worthless items.

Which is what it was.

Worthless.

Worthless-except-to-me.

But unlike like a doorknob, an elevator button, a nudie mag, a soda, if I told anyone 'Look at this' then confessed it was so spectacular I needed it to be mine they'd feel no kindred flame.

They'd not see why.

Would tell me to buy it.

Offer to gift me it.

Be glad I'd discovered something which meant so much to me and which they'd been happy to provide.

I couldn't stomach the notion of anyone knowing I'd *discovered* it, even. Anything which might make it less *exclusively* mine was unconscionable.

No traditional circumstance could satisfy the criterion for my truly possessing the *Jademan Kung-Fu Special*.

Did it belong to the store?

In the teleological sense?

The store'd bought it, of course. Along with whichever items else in some shipment. Even if it'd been included complimentary, the fact they'd needed to purchase other items for such opportunity to present itself gave them Earthly rights to the thing.

No sentences I might speak, no syllogism I might proffer, would lead to my friends, the shopkeepers, letting me have it for nothing.

I'd never dream of asking them to.

Why should they?

They'd stand correct in all they'd explain about supply, demand, transactional ownership.

Things any dolt knew.

The risk of alienation was the correct cost.

Betraying my friends made sense as price-tag.

I giggled and daydreamed of the volume's front cover.

Down in the corner a value listed.

In US currency: *One Soul*.

In Canadian: *One Soul twenty-five*.

On the day of the theft my head pulsed. A globe stuffed full of eyes held wide and crusted. The skin of my arms seemed strained with dozens of ears subcutaneous. My veins had a slow current, like air breathed through a nosebleed.

I'd gone to the back corner too often in recent days.

I could sense it.

Going again was what the authorities were waiting for.

This was a television episode.

A sting was underway.

Every customer lingering was waiting for their cue to flash a badge, pull a pistol.

The neighboring establishments would open their doors to reveal interiors empty except for officers in tactical gear, technicians manning the reel-to-reel recorders which'd captured the audio-visual evidence to be presented before a Grand Jury by lunch time.

For the task, I'd dressed in the baggy black pants best suited. The freshest, tightest, cleanest socks I owed.

I wrapped the issue around my shin.

Secured it.

Stood.

A casual glance to the door didn't show it receding like a camera trick.

Patrons' faces didn't warp as though filmed with fish-eye lens or presented in funhouse glass.

The door was just there.

Seemed closer than usual.

Opened already.

A getaway driver.

Engine purring.

Cigarette about to be tossed from the window.

Radio waiting to blare.

I started leafing through various back-issues in the alphabetized boxes on the long countertop. Titles I'd never heard of. Had no interest in.

I starred. Unseeing. Cavefish.

Would the *Jademan Kung-Fu Special* loosen from where I'd fit it?

Certainly a possibility.

Never before had I lingered so long when employing this technique.

There'd been occasion when hidden skin mags had flopped free from our legs while Alain and I trekked one end of the Shopping Center to the other. Fop sweat had collapsed us to our knees. We'd scrambled to concoct gestures which might disguise slipping the contraband out, curling it under arms. Hastened away. Already outside. Already free. Croupy laughter in barking echo off brick walls, glass windows, tornadoing skyward.

I stood.

Waiting for something.

But not for disaster.

Everything going wrong would be an acceptable outcome. I'd shook the hand of Fate on that count from Go.

It didn't yet make sense to leave.

Something hadn't occurred to me to do.

An insomniac sensation that the proper gesture to lock the world down hadn't been found.

Said.

Done.

I took up a random title from the back-issue bins. To this day, I've no idea what it was.

It puzzles me how neither of the proprietors made a comment, asked a question. They knew me, my tastes. So often gabbed about my selections, cracking wise or shooting recommendations for alternatives.

I remember nothing like that while I paid, this day.

What I remember is the item was purchased for eleven dollars, fifty-five cents.

I tendered the money.

Money which wasn't mine.

Traded the money for something I never wanted while stealing something I did.

It was money they'd never have received otherwise.

I recall as well how they asked did I mind five-cents of the forty-five cents change being pennies. They'd no more dimes. Down to three nickels. It was pennies or I could wait for one of them to get back from breaking a bill next door at the Grog.

Pennies were fine.

At the trashcan beside the payphone near the stairs leading out of the Shopping Center, I discarded whatever I'd bought. Dropped the coins, slick with clammy palm moisture, vaguely to the pavement.

I'd not allow myself to catch even peripheral glimpse of the *Kung-Fu Special* as I walked.

I shouldn't look at it.

Even once.

Never open it.

Be ignorant forever of its content.

The scent of its pages.

I ought never know a single thing more than what I already knew from the image of it recollected from back in that advertisement.

It existed.

It looked like this.

It was mine.

Coming to the Post Office, I stopped.

Stood at the mail collection bin, holding the comic.

My sopping fingers would've warped the gloss of its cover if not for the thin plastic sheath the item was bagged in.

I dropped it inside.

Then unburdened, complete, I continued home.

I thought to myself as I walked 'What had it felt like, doing that?'

It'd felt like not being me.

I thought to myself, later, at night, in bed, unasleep 'What had that felt like, not being you?'

It'd felt like being me.

'And what do I feel like?' I asked myself, sometime later.

I should know. Knew I should know.

Knew not being me felt like being me.

Knew being me felt like not being me.

'Shouldn't you feel like both of those, then?' I asked.

But I felt like neither.

So didn't answer myself.

.2.

I'D SPENT THE DURATION OF seventh-grade's final field-trip regurgitating tangy bile over the rail of a fishing boat. All witnesses took pains to make this an experience I'd never forget.

The summer had given the oral history of the event ample room to breathe. By opening day of eighth-grade, other bodily fluids had been woven into the Maritain tale.

Quite the sea shanty I made for.

A day wouldn't go by without my being accosted by some plucky cub reporter looking to score a scoop.

Not often was there captive chance to interview the Elephant Man.

How had it felt to puke, urinate, and soil myself with diarrhea simultaneous?

My leprous reputation wasn't aided by the fact that not only were we still required to change clothes for Gym class but it was now against regulation to wear one's sweatpants throughout the day.

Faculty had their eyes peeled to catch rascals like me who'd double up, sporting Gym outfits underneath regular outerwear in order to flout this regulation.

I'd duck into one of the locker room's toilet cubicles to change.

This tactic led to me being pegged a *fairy*. Or rather, it reinforced a limp wrist being considered canon for my character.

I attempted to prevail upon my classmates with logic.

Were I hot to drink in their underoos or gander at their splendid appendages, wouldn't I use the locker room policy to be living the high life?

But my detractors would pivot to logic their own.

I was the one talking like a bigot.

Was I meaning to imply there was some reason to be concerned about being queer?

I'd retort how, whether or not I was homosexual, it was the spit flicked at me from passing fingertips in the corridors I was trying to avoid.

So according to me: I was locking myself in the stall because I was gay, knew they weren't, and understood what'd be coming my way if they caught me making sneaky peeks?

Couldn't trust myself not to, eh?

Hid away to subdue my raging urges?

It was exactly like they'd been saying, then. I should stop being so defensive.

Every color of the rainbow, right?

Even had I managed to sway the crowd with further argument it'd soon've proved moot.

Due to my efforts trying to get out of a pin in a wrestling bout required for a passing grade my goose was cooked.

All my classmates in a circle.

Watching my hips buck up vigorously while I'd squirmed beneath my opponent.

Here was the smoking gun everyone needed.

Stop press.

For someone who claimed up-and-down he didn't even want to participate in wrestling, Jasper sure hadn't taken steps to end the match any sooner than necessary.

I spouted off at my tormentors one afternoon.

Did they have any idea how much pornography I'd stolen in my life?

'Listen to the overcompensation going on' came the chorus.

Come to mention it, the next verse began, that was common knowledge. As was what I'd done to the stuff when I'd realized Alain hadn't been looking for a boyfriend.

I explained I wouldn't touch Alain with Alain's.

They replied they believed me.

That's what I had my own for, right?

Rinse. Repeat.

Rinse.

Repeat.

I'd do my best to miss at least two out of the five days in a school week. Three if I could manage it. The whole week were it shortened already by holiday.

Promptly I learned this had consequences even more dire.

I was summoned to the Guidance Office one afternoon. No warning.

I figured it was to do with attendance, my slipping grades. Figured I'd have to start turning things around. Resigned myself to such fate while I plopped in the waiting area.

I'd show up.

Toe the line.

Grit through.

Start taking it on the chin.

The last thing I wanted was for matters to escalate into trouble at home.

The counselor took me to a private office inside the office proper. Cozy but somber. It felt like I was only in a diorama of where I was.

She adopted what on television would indicate a maternal air.

Asked how I was doing.

Trying on puckishness, I went with 'I figure that's what I'm here for you to tell me.'

A television script would say: *The counselor smiled warmly. Beat. Took a breath. Beat. Leaned in.*

She wanted me to understand how I wasn't in any kind of trouble.

Whatever we talked about was private.

Would be held in confidence.

'I find that hard to believe' I didn't say while saying 'It's fine, doesn't matter.'

Who cooked dinner at home?

My mom?

My blood crinkled like slowly uncoiling cellophane. I swallowed a breath textured like a golf ball. Explained my mom cooked when she could. She worked a lot, though. My dad sometimes made hamburgers or beefsteak. I liked those. I'd also cook for myself. Knew how. Canned pasta. Sausage links. There weren't a lot of things me and my brothers would eat, so it hardly mattered who cooked.

It'd been noticed I never ate at school. Or at least that I ate nothing but salt packets.

Could I shed some light on that?

'I don't like school lunch. I eat at home. The salt's for a laugh. The kids I sit with get a kick out of it. It's not any more salt than they put on their food, just looks more interesting taken straight.'

Your mom or dad don't pack you lunch?

'My dad gives me money. I don't like the lunch here. I like keeping the money.'

You don't give the money back?

Do you save it up?

Do you use it for anything?

'Sometimes I use it. For food. Or whatever. Just not here. I save some, too.'

You wear more than one layer of clothes, even in the warmer weather. Long sleeved.

Aren't you hot?

Is it uncomfortable?

'I don't like changing in front of classmates. I don't want anyone looking at me.'

Why was I being called to account for my every peccadillo?

I could feel myself draining of color, shape, size. My entire physicality flattened to the back of my skull. My eyes were like twin keyhole apertures looking out through murky water.

I was told it seemed I was sick quite a lot.

Was there a diagnosis?

I never seemed to go to the doctor.

My dad was a doctor, I explained. He wrote me notes.

I was told that while my dad's notes always excused my absences, they never really stated what was wrong.

When I presented notes.

When those notes seemed genuine.

Needing no weather man to know which way this wind was blowing, I went with the only tactic left.

First, I verified whether she was going to tell my parents about all this, for real. When she reiterated she couldn't do that unless I told her she could, I broke out in tears.

Admitted it was a sham.

I wasn't sick.

Hardly ever was.

I faked it.

Fooled my dad.

Forged the notes.

I just didn't like school.

I'd rather stay home.

'People have noticed. Your classmates are concerned about you.'

My classmates hated me.
What did they tell her about me?
'We're concerned about you. Is everything alright? At home?'
Everything's fine at home, I blubbered.
Why else did she think I wanted to stay there?
'Is there anything you want to tell me about home?'
I asked if I could leave. I was sorry. Reiterated she wasn't to tell my dad I forged notes. Assured her my mom fed me fine. Did everything she could think of for me. She just had to work all the time. I'd come to class like I was supposed to. I just didn't like anybody. I was fine. Everything was.
A week, two, however many passed by.
I remember nothing of them but waiting out clocks and struggling to catch up on assignments for which there seemed no purpose.
I was acutely aware of every praise from a teacher.
Suspected them all.
Wondered how my responses would be summarized in the dossier being compiled.
In English class, especially, came offers again which had come before. I could be moved into the high-level courses the teacher thought I belonged in. If I would show the same talent in my graded assignments which came through in the extra-credit work. The journals. The poetry.
It was always a mistake to think I was meant to respond with honesty. To reveal myself.
To admit I rather liked the lower classes.
Explain it wasn't indicative of aspiration on my part that I read the books I'd write reports on for extra-points whilst ignoring the ones assigned.
The latter were fine enough.
The former were things I was randomly reading anyway, why not cash in?

The writing in the journals was simply different, spiritually, than the writing for the assignments.

The talents weren't of a kind.

I merely had one variety of skill. No interest in having the other.

I learned to say 'Okay.'

To reply to any teachers' well-meaning sentiments as though the words of praise they spoke were worth the paper they were printed on.

I could feel the world regaining equilibrium.

A storm had passed.

The surface of the Earth was cooling to allow for evolution.

NO IDEA WHY HE PULLED me from the flotsam, but in the midst of my travails I wound up with a buddy.

I called him *Dan the Trekkie*.

There's every chance his name was something altogether unlike *Dan*. Didn't seem to matter. Probably how our friendship sustained. Him not asking me to explain myself. Me not offering to.

Dan was a kid who without blush would ask a teacher to leave a projector slide up longer on account of his stodgy eyesight made it take forever to copy notes. Despite this, he wasn't cursed to wander beneath overcast skies. In no sense was he popular, but got on well with the general populace. Physical traits, statements, habits for which I'd have been thumped often garnered him chumminess from those I considered predators. Quirks which would've marked me for sterilization left him miraculously unscathed.

I was loathe to let Dan in on who, on what I was. If he'd been the sort to show interest in anything scofflaw, it would've been me who'd put the nix to our interacting. I'd have fronted off how I wasn't the type to go in for uncouth misadventures.

I was in no head to trust another criminal.

In no head to trust someone who'd trust me if they were given fair chance.

I needed a friend who'd want nothing to do with me were we actually friends.

Life was different for thieves.

Friendship wasn't predicated on intimacy.

It was based on concealment.

One party harbored a secret. Preferably a volatile one the other didn't ever catch sniff of.

Undercover Customs Agent and wine smuggler.

Mob mole and G-Man.

Dan was what I wanted to be. He lived with the invisibility of room temperature.

I wasn't a bit like him. Lived with the invisibility of an odor.

*Star Trek* was the glue of our bond. *Captain Picard, Data, Q*.

We liked the original series, the motion pictures well enough, too. But it was the twenty-fourth century rather than the twenty-third where we most naturally dwelt.

Anywhere but the twentieth like the curs we moved amongst.

Meeting Dan was propitious, seeing as my love for things *Trek* had only recently hit full tilt.

On Bookstore trips, my dad could be convinced to buy me novels, novelizations. He'd even willingly purchased a dictionary of the *Klingon* language. Quite a surprise. I'd figured he'd have thought it frivolous. To the contrary. Some colleagues of his had been involved in the development of *Esperanto*, back in the day. I'd find him leafing through the volume, himself, in spare moments.

Whenever my mom gifted me something it'd be *Trek* related.

Playsets.

Toy gadgets.

VHS tapes.

She even chaperoned me to a fan convention. Sprang for a

child-sized uniform and a prop which had allegedly been used on film.

A *Klingon* dagger. Crafted out of some kind of rough, low-grade polypropylene.

I wondered at the pedigree of this collectable. Despite its Certificate of Authenticity.

The more scrutiny I gave the matter, the more disenchanted I became.

The blades in the flicks sure looked of genuine metal.

Perhaps my item had been utilized by a background performer. No need for a full level of realism.

It made sense the object I possessed hadn't been important. It'd cost my mom a good amount, but hardly a fortune.

Likely had never appeared on camera.

Yard Sale backwash.

Those sellers could've been hucksters, really.

How hard could it be to do up these replicas?

The Certificates?

*A prop with authentic workmanship ... as used in ...*

Such glorious weasel speak.

I could spend half-hour down at any Copy Shop doctoring up such documentation.

What customer would bother to check on the veracity of such things?

To which authority would they appeal?

Thinking back, sometimes it's strange to me the energies expended to assure I'd *not* treasure this item.

Almost with shame I admit I came to regret having it. Lost track of it more quickly than I would've some fast-food tossaway trinket.

Other times the reason for the effort seems plain.

Real of fake, I hadn't stolen the prop.

I should've.

Never ought to've allowed it to diminish in intrigue by being mine legally.

If there'd been a gyp, the fast-one should've been mine.

The possible inauthenticity of the dagger exposed me to the risk of being seen the sucker. A thief with no nose for the Art I practiced.

Most of my money, ill-got or otherwise, went to the subject of *Trek*, as well.

At the Comic Shop I plonked down cash for an unopened box of forty packs of collectable cards. The proprietors tried directing me to full collections of the card series, already assembled. Pristine condition. Explained I wasn't even guaranteed to come up with a full set from random packs. Plus, the pre-made sets would cost less than the box I was springing for.

But I was after something altogether different.

I was buying myself *joy*.

Trading hard currency for the ability to peacefully sit, playacting shopkeeper and customer. Serene in a world where I inhabited every role.

I was paying to experience forty trips to the shop as some regular kid might.

Forty weeks' worth of allowances for chores.

Three months of hope and excitement as my collection assembled.

All in the span of one day.

I was getting my hands on the most succulent parts of an ordinary life, snug in the monastery of my bedroom.

Sorting through cards eight at-a-time, I was thrilled by every duplicate. Such horrible suspense, thinking I'd wind up with the set in full. What a catastrophe that'd be. Gutting to come out on top.

I gave one of every duplicate card to Dan.

He was well pleased. Insisted on paying me.

I told him it couldn't be less important. These dupes would've been chucked in the bin if it hadn't occurred to me he might like them.

The next day he brought me fifteen dollars.

I protested, refused to accept it.

In that case, he passed back the cards I'd given him.

'Dan, please. I want you to have them.'

'Then take the money.'

I had no way out of it.

Very amused with himself, Dan asked whether I had any clue how collecting was meant to work. Fella should always keep one set of something for their own. Another set should be maintained to trade or sell with.

Get it?

I didn't get it, no. Nor could I have cared less.

But he seemed chuffed to make me wise, so I listened.

Collectors kept duplicates for sundry reasons.

Autographs, for example.

Other collectors'd pay fifty times what a pack cost for one single card, given proper conditions.

Take his brother who'd spent three-hundred bucks for a hockey card.

He'd had the same card, already. The three-hundred was for the card signed by the goalie it depicted.

That evening, I tore around my bedroom. Dug through the mess of loose papers, comic books, paperbacks, action figures, miscellany, and scores of half-empty *Gatorade* bottles I'd let build to a thick clutter on all surfaces.

Included with promotional materials at the *Trek* convention had been a flier with a reproduction of William Shatner's autograph on it.

I was so relieved my packrat nature had saved this trifle I now had acute purpose for.

I spent the next week trying my hand at forgery.

Felt I'd got the chicken-scratch down pat.

Noia kicked in.

Mustn't get ahead of myself. Savvy folks knew people like me littered this world. Always setting out snares to obstruct us.

The reproduction autograph on the promo appeared as though written in thick silver marker.

I didn't trust it.

Likely it was baked into Shatner's contracts how his valuable penmanship couldn't be machined by any fly-by-night operation churning out disposable faff.

Probably there was an official false signature. A stamp. Telltale differences which'd keep the unscrupulous from running riot.

I leaned on the Comic Shop display case, squinting down at various autographed items. Stroke of luck, they had some memorabilia signed by cast members of classic *Trek*.

Headshot of *Captain Kirk*.

Shatner's name scribbled in thin pen.

Didn't look principally different than on the flier.

I bought the photograph, regardless.

Along with three packs of original series trading cards.

The glossy stock made it tricky to get a clean scribble down. A thin, felt-tip marker worked best. But looked a tad fake. I'd have preferred a pen which'd indent the card face a bit. There'd be a genuineness to that.

I signed every card without Shatner's picture on it as practice.

Then every card depicting him.

Held the fugazies beside the real deal.

Imagined severe scrutiny would be given the sig.

At lunch, I presented Dan with the card. Prim in a stiff plastic sheath.

'It's a gift' I made clear. Not a trade. Not a sale.

He was over the moon to have it.

But was I certain?

He couldn't imagine I'd had this laying around.

How much had it cost?

Didn't matter. Stop with the questions.

I explained I wanted it to be his. It was important to me. I'd worked hard to procure the thing for him.

Kept my phrasings loose. Didn't want to tell a literal lie.

I simply wanted him to accept the gesture.

Because he was my friend.

NOTHING EVER GOES AWAY. THAT'S one lesson. It's entirely my fault everything doesn't. That's another. Because I never do anything to make anything.

This third lesson was the most important.

Was also the one I seemed least invested in learning.

In medias res: Me, arriving home from school. My mom needs to speak with me.

What on Earth did I have to say for myself about the 'goddamned pharmacy' she'd found beneath my bed?

A priori: Despite my stated preferences she leave things lay, my mom had taken it upon herself to give my bedroom a thorough cleanse.

Every pill I'd pretended to swallow the previous year had been discovered.

Her concerns were with regard to how if I didn't take the medications, I'd not get better.

All these days of school I'd missed.

How behind I'd keep getting.

Sincere concerns.

Valid.

Misguided.

She didn't deduce the underlying deceit.

Clearly I wasn't going to front-off this pill situation was reasonable. It wasn't my style to protest when caught red-handed.

However, with months of school yet remaining, I couldn't cop to the full facts.

It was a tricky situation.

Whatever I'd said, I'd got it over with quick.

Mea cupla. I'd turn this ship around.

So immediately I undertook a bracing reflection on my character.

I was some piece of work.

How had the hands on the clock come to this?

Laziness, pure and simple.

After cheeking, palming, pocketing, what I'd do was keep the medicine tablets on my person until laying abed. Slip them down the space between my mattress side and bedroom wall. Consider them lost to the subterranean clutter. Never give them a second thought.

Really idiotic. Showcasing a complete lack of foresight.

Yet I wasn't without foresight. Far from it.

I'd keep up the affect of being a sickly sort throughout the summer months.

I was the polar opposite of idiotic.

Knew schemes would fall flat if I only played invalid come the school year.

I possessed keen intelligence. Laid complex groundwork. Used my allergies and irritable bowels to my advantage. At times purposefully ingested foodstuffs which'd induce suffering. I'd fake taking proper medication, liquid form, for sneezing, mucus, watery eyes, willingly suffering the results. Make it seem the severity of my affliction was beyond the reaches of over-the-counter science.

Middle of July I'd sometimes force myself to puke in earshot of my dad or mom then spend a day or two in bed.

Television.
Peanut butter crackers.
*Gatorade.*
The promise of the peace I'd later require.
I noted the plump irony in what I'd been caught at versus what I hadn't.
My room was litterbugged with crime. Evidence dense as jungle brush. The pills ought to've been the least troubling discovery.
Paperbacks, model ships, art supplies by the bushel.
Movies, snack foods, and all sorts of nevermind.
Most of all, there was a grand larceny of *Star Trek* action figures. Now neatly arranged by my mom's hand into a container set atop the otherwise cleared-off dresser. A veritable rogue's gallery of poseable figurines.
Why so many?
Greed?
Compulsion?
Hardly. These were essentials to a well-balanced life.
My habit was to play sprawling, labyrinthine games with the toys. Days freed of school I'd live out episodes of such craft and minutia that to relate in full a single one would make a listener dizzy.
Intricate plots.
Rich in symbolism and philosophical quandary.
Developed arcs to every character.
Twists.
Turns.
Once elements of a game were set in motion, no deus ex machina could be initiated. Every line of thought and consequence would be explored to novelistic terminus, good or ill. Subplots would examine tweaks and iterations of every tale's primary thesis.

It'd not be going too far to say the bulk of my social development and outlooks on life were drawn from the fictive exploits of these purloined space adventurers.

My mom had sprung for certain items.

The Transporter playset.

The Shuttlecraft.

The expensive set of original-cast figures displayed on replica of the old-school *Enterprise* bridge.

But the fifty other figures and sundry extras had been shoplifted.

It'd become habitual.

My jaunt through the fence behind the motel.

Across train tracks.

My stroll past the fairgrounds.

Plundering the Toy Store located halfway to the mall.

My system was ritualistic.

The circuit of aisles I'd walk while cutting packs, wresting free figures and accessories.

Where I'd slip items to pockets or duffle bag.

Where I'd ditch the gutted packaging.

When I'd learned the door to the public restroom was neither alarmed nor had camera pointed toward it I'd become brazen.

Took items in.

Prised them open at my leisure.

Boxes would be disposed of in the toilet trash.

No twit, I'd cut the cardboard to pieces. These pieces I'd stuff inside fast-food bags I'd then bury down the receptacle's bowels.

I'd be cautious to exit the lavatory with a few untampered boxes. Just in case.

My life, writ large, was little more than waiting for someone in authority to tell me to empty my pockets.

My conclusion was it could be no other way.

I'd no inclination to not be found out, forever.

That'd be goofy.

When there was reasonable way to talk myself out of or wriggle free from being apprehended, of course I'd do my able best.

But once I was bang-to-rights?

I'd nothing to say for myself my actions hadn't already articulated.

It simply remained to experience what'd come next.

Learn what people would tolerate.

Worst come of worse, I'd be punished. Dismissed.

It was out of my hands whether an association with a person or place was continued. Under which conditions.

I was a thief so I thieved.

People could take me or leave me.

Were I a composer and someone took a disliking to that, would I cease compositions at their disappointed behest?

Rubbish.

I was at peace with being known for precisely what I was if such identity organically came to light.

The world, however, seemed bent on trumping up its own narratives.

I'd arrived at school late, one day. Fit myself to the lunch table beside Dan. He gave me a wary side-eye.

Had I forged the William Shatner autograph?

My mind flitted through files, triple-time.

What could be the source of such query?

Maybe my mentioning forging notes from my dad?

But when had that ever come up?

'Not on the card I gave you' I shrugged offhand. 'But I know how to forge it. A little trick I've learnt.'

Could probably counterfeit his sig if it'd amuse him.

That was okay. He wanted me to have the card back, though.

I insisted there was no call to get silly. The autograph on his card was bona fide. It's what I'd taught myself from.

Seemingly non-sequitur, he told me the Creative Writing teacher was really mad at me.

This didn't compute.

Creative Writing was the only class I made any effort in. Made spectacular efforts, truth be told. I expounded this fact to Dan.

Well, the teacher'd given a long talk about me to the other students. Laying out her theory that I was a plagiarist. Used me as an example of shaky artistic ethics. Wanted to see me at my earliest convenience. Since I was a tough man to get a hold of, she'd asked Dan to put a tickle in my ear when next we crossed paths.

Catching the teacher during her lunch period while meantime I should've been in Social Studies I demanded 'What's this about plagiarism?'

Hadn't my work been exemplary?

I turned in fifteen pages when an assignment required two. Abstracted luscious conceptual turns from the rote prompts given me.

Didn't my stories and poems explore life in ways which illuminated many fantastic things?

This was her point. No other kid wrote anything remotely like what I wrote. The denseness, complexity, craft, stylistics were far beyond what was discussed in class. Almost preposterously above grade-level.

'Where exactly is it I'm supposed to have plagiarized *from*?'

Now hold my horses. She didn't want to get off on a wrong foot.

In truth, she'd spent a good amount of time looking into the matter. She'd uncovered no specific text I'd cribbed from.

But she'd shared my work with many of my teachers who had agreed it was of suspicious quality considering my observed habits and what was turned in to them.

Even my English teacher, who I'd have thought would've gone to bat for me, had reconsidered her theory that I was gifted. Based on journals and extra-credit assignments, it seemed so. But those were composed off-premises. The work for the class done under real-time observation was wildly different. As was the quality of writing in projects I'd turned in for other classes even with weeks to prepare them, outside of school.

Not unamused, I asked how was I to prove I'd done what I'd done. A neat variant on my usual preoccupation with possibly having to prove I hadn't done what I had.

The teacher asked some questions about where I got my ideas, where I'd come across certain techniques and flourishes.

Flustered and on the spot, I didn't have pat answers to deliver.

'I just make the stuff up' I said. 'I read books. Watch television. There's influence, I suppose.'

But I'd no idea where specific ideas *came* from.

She was at a loss. Admitted it.

However, my answers didn't cut muster.

Too many things failed to add up.

She'd done her homework, didn't I see?

Had learned, to put it cutely, I never did mine.


I ARRIVED AT THE CONVENTION decked out in the colors of *Lieutenant Commander Data*. Had somehow convinced my mom to drop me off then come back at the end of the day. My duffle bag was hefty with purloined *Trek* novels tarted up with imitation William Shatner autographs.

Big plans. Great big plans.

But an entire corner of auditorium was dedicated to autograph dealers.

Shatner sigs were dime-a-dozen.

These pros had behind-the-scenes images with witticisms scribbled on them. Shooting scripts buckshot with notations. Entire letters written by the man.

What good was a bilked paperback with my hastily rendered scribble on it going to do me, here?

I tried to work a few exchanges with non-autograph dealers.

That action figure for this signed copy of *World Without End*?

Mostly got plain Naws.

Though one degenerate swindler said he'd take two bucks off something if I threw in a book. Trying to take advantage of a child.

Sidled up to random fans as they made their rounds.

Gravitated toward kids my own age.

They'd have to check with their mothers?

Nevermind.

One ponytailed fellow, late teens, earlier twenties, Sherlock Holmesed one of my books thoroughly before declining any transaction.

I saw this guy then make for the autograph tables.

Observed him squinting at various photos on display.

Watched him strike up a chat with some vendor.

When that scene finished off, he gave a slow glance around as though aiming to point me out.

I felt like a crumb caught in my own lip crease.

I'd really reckoned to turn a profit. Instead, my stint as a peddler of counterfeits was already kaput.

I'd no money for anything worthwhile. Only'd brought enough to buy a doodad or two for appearances.

Hours to go until my mom would collect me.

Straight theft was all that remained.

But this was complicated by Dan meeting me at noon. Something arranged months previous to our schism. We'd remained paly, but our interactions had become fewer. Were friends over phone-wires through plate-glass.

Dan being in the area made me self-conscious about stealing.

More-and-more I worked to loosen our orbit.

He'd be looking at some item. I'd chat a few words. Move off to look at something else. Move a bit further. Free roam. Return to him. Chat a few words.

Repeat.

Thankfully, he didn't mind when I begged off some Question and Answer event he was set on attending.

I recall the lifts I made being almost unthinking.

I'd set the plastic bag containing my few legitimate purchases on top of the items-for-sale spread across the folding tables while I playacted browsing.

When I'd lift the bag, whichever item I was grifting I'd pin behind it.

Simply turn to the folding table on the other side of me. Set the bag down.

Wait a beat.

Suddenly act as though looking for something inside it.

In doing so, I'd unearth the legitimately purchased items.

Returning them to the bag, I'd slip in the item purloined.

Whereupon I'd turn back to the original table.

Ask the dealer a question about the price of something.

Thank them.

Move slowly on.

It was as though I'd melded with the surrounding commotion. The same strangers who could ruin my life with an odd drift of focus and a penchant for civics served as my protective sheath.

After all, who'd think some kid so flagrant they'd steal while elbow-to-elbow with three women dressed as competing version of *Uhura* and a half-dozen men debating the finer points of warp coils?

After every few burglings, I'd snake hotel corridors not designated for *Trek* festivities. Unload all illegitimately owned items from plastic bag to duffle.

Eventually Dan wandered back to have a gab with me.

I had plastic bag chock full of contraband-awaiting-transfer in one hand. Duffle in the other. Heavy enough it strained my wrist to carry.

We'd agreed to watch a Costume Contest together when a man who clearly wielded authority approached with a dealer in tow.

They needed to speak to us.

Before I could manage a meep to spare Dan from being dragged into so hideous an affair, the dealer piped up how it was only me he'd meant.

Dan met my eyes.

I shrugged. Told him I'd see him in a sec. 'Save me a seat.'

This dealer had the sinking suspicion I'd stolen a graphic novel from his table.

I certainly had.

Trouble was, that theft had been some time ago. The book now tucked inside my duffle with ten-zillion other things.

It was all fresh steal in the plastic bag I was presently to permit the man-in-authority to poke through. That being the last thing I'd find permissible, I began a hasty tap dance.

'Which graphic novel?'

Oh, yeah. I had that. But hadn't stolen it.

'Hold on.'

Went to my knees. Opened the duffle. Careful not to allow them a solid glimpse inside.

'Is this it?'

The dealer identified it as his specific copy by a clever mark to the inside cover.

Well, I was as shocked as anyone.

Coming to think of it, however, I might be the true victim in all this. While I hadn't bought the thing, I had made a trade for it.

'What did you trade?'

No beat skipped, I answered with hyper-specifics.

'Figure of *Captain Kirk* in a kind of space-parachute suit.' As

I understood it, the getup was from a never-filmed sequence in *Star Trek: Generations*. Or one cut because it'd looked silly. 'Either way, I bought a comic adaptation which'd included the scene. Thought it neat there'd been a toy produced.' However, I'd opted to have the graphic novel the guy offered over the collectable figure when given the chance.

This made exquisite sense to both of them.

The man-in-authority concurred it all tracked. The trade-value would've been equivalent.

Yep, the dealer would drink to that.

They both sure were sorry, but I still had to relinquish the book.

The dealer frowned how it sucked I'd come up short, but he couldn't give his goods away.

'I more than understand. Don't give it another thought.'

Concurrent to realizing how dunderheaded my dodge had been, the man-in-authority politely requested I come talk to someone else.

I was certain our destination was the table from which I'd actually yoinked the very *Kirk* I'd only moments before described.

My wits limply fritzed.

No way out of the briar patch, now.

But we wandered over to the autograph tables.

A particular vendor was flagged.

Man-in-authority pointed at me.

Was I the guy?

I seized up.

Autograph dealer waved dismissive. Naw. Guy he'd meant had been older. Ponytail.

Man-in-authority intimated how there'd been complaints of some chucklehead trying to pass bogus sigs. Do trades. Probably the same shyster who'd hustled me.

'Yeah yeah' I murmured 'yeah, a ponytail.' Guy who'd traded me had a ponytail. 'As a matter of fact, he'd asked did I want some autographed stuff. Told him I'd talk to *legitimate* vendors if I did'.

'Smart' the man-in-authority nodded with a sigh. 'Sounds like our man, anyway.'

If they caught him, they'd get my toy back for me.

I'd sure appreciate that.

Numb, I exited the Dealer's room.

Dan was standing nervously by. He'd skipped the Costume Contest.

What had happened?

Was I okay?

On edge, unable to simply demur or invent a random scenario, I groused how some conjob working the convention had stolen something then traded it to me for a toy I'd had.

'Which toy?'

I noticed Dan noticing the heftiness of my plastic bag. My duffle. 'Some *Kirk* I bought, earlier.'

His face loosened. Grew confused. 'I thought you didn't have money for stuff, today'.

'Enough for that toy …' I waffled '… was pretty much how much'.

What was in my bag, then?

'Listen, Dan … I have to use the toilet.'

Those were the final words to ever pass between us.

After them I recall the crippling weight of being cognizant of his gaze on me as I trod the thin corridor toward the escalators feeding down to the entry plaza of the lavish hotel. To this day I can hear the verdant blood writhing, clogged within my ears, its thumping louder than the petulant cackle of that soaring lobby fountain. It often seems to me the leaky scents of mayonnaise and flatulent sauerkraut which slouched across the lobby air inside steam from the slow-cookers of frankfurter vendors permanently imbued my skin that day.

I pushed through the door of a palatial lavatory. Black-and-white and faux-marble. Cold air the fragrance of genuine lime.

Closed in the furthest cubicle, I started empting my plastic bag into the wall-mounted trash-receptacle.

Then became calm.

Huffed a dubious chuckled.

I could simply abandon my duffle.

With the plastic bag inside it.

Leave everything on the toilet floor.

Walk away.

Free.

Each minute of the two hours before my mom showed up I felt further away from the world. Decades removed from my crimes of only moments previous.

I knew myself as who I was. Where I was. What I was.

But not from *when* I was.

Knew myself as though a story which'd been told me years ago, as though a story which'd be related only in years yet to come, from some moment further along than even me telling this, now.

Knew myself as from my past, looking forward, as from my future, looking back.

I was just watching.

What had happened. What would.

Blissfully indifferent to either.

A glee. A giggle. A guilty.

.part three.

.1.

WHO WOULDN'T SPARE A KID a quarter to use the public telephone?

Dressed in my school uniform?

'I've been waiting on my ride for half-hour, just need to give them a call.'

I'd have purposefully told my dad the bus home from school dropped me off an hour later than it would. Would use the interim to loiter while customers exited, flush with change from their burger purchases.

'Excuse me, I'm fifty-cents short of a sausage biscuit. My dad's running late. Got a coin or two?'

Folks might help me without thinking twice.

I'd hit one up.

Head inside while they drove away.

Wait five minutes.

Loiter out front.

Hit up another.

Few bucks a day. Could be fun.

I thought about this plan every morning when left off by my dad at the fast-food joint. Refined the daydream on the school bus while it hauled me and a dozen other kids forty-five minutes to the private Catholic school where my mom had me enrolled.

The school had been a dynamite idea on her part. Meant to turn things around for me after the middle-school harrows. Keep me from dwelling beneath a bridge at least until I was of legal age.

I loved everything about the place.

My uniform.

The only-two-hundred-students total, ninth-grade-through-twelfth.

The morning prayers.

The Friday liturgies.

The sacrament I was disallowed.

The courses and services conducted in the converted rooms of a Civil War era mansion, a slipshod gymnasium, and a clutter of portable classrooms nestled at the overgrown edge of a shabby stamp of woodland.

Love notwithstanding, I spent the first month almost stone silent, lunch periods huddled in a toilet stall.

The assumption I was queer for doing so was amusing, now, rather than intimidating. The assertion of my classmates wasn't malicious. Their suspicion rather tender.

A homosexual was nothing my new peers might ridicule. At the very worst, discussing their take on my predilections was a venue for them to proffer glib platitudes on the inclusivity of Christ and whatnot.

So I ran with it.

I was a queer as much I was an anything.

My skeletal frame carried some of my mom's now vintage dresses beautifully. My eyelashes had always made women envious. My lips had taken on the plush of strawberry flesh which a careful application of flavored balm would scrumptiously accent.

There weren't many opportunities to show any of this off on school grounds, but I seized every one.

Halloween.

Prize days for school spirit.

A girl I'd taken a shine to was disappointed by the spreading word of my orientation. I learned this from a note passed to me.

I didn't much see the conflict.

I went both ways, for all I knew.

Not to mention, had she seen her red hair, her freckles, her pallor?

When I spelled things out that way, she was chuffed. Had really liked my dress, too, by the way.

We went on one date. My first ever.

Strange and hollow.

Sublime.

I'd figured to impress her upon arrival to the Movie Theater by spontaneously announcing there'd be no need for tickets. I was crackerjack at sneaking into flicks.

So happened this was entirely true.

Though I'd have gone with the line even if it hadn't been.

There'd be no need for that. Her friend worked there. Would let us in.

Prepared for such eventuality, I'd come loaded up with loot. Offered to lavish snack foods on her like some Hollywood magnate.

Again, all covered by her pal.

Plus, she wasn't much for a sweet-tooth.

Left to merely watching the movie and hanging around, I felt unimpressive. Hadn't a word to say for myself except about what I could've bought or stolen her. Everything to do with me seemed certain to bore her dreadfully.

Tried mentioning how I'd wander about like a hobo a lot. Panhandle. Sleep out-of-doors some nights for kicks.

To add some texture, tossed in how while I wandered I'd take photographs with a manual camera. Had been inspired by the television series *Nowhere Man*.

Was she a fan?

Never heard of the show.

But she really liked the trench coat I'd sometimes wear.

Pity. I didn't much care for that trench coat. It'd simply been the only one the Department Store had sold. I'd decided to stop wearing it, entirely.

She wasn't very boisterous about herself, so I couldn't showcase my ace listening skills.

The obviously-not-naturally-red hair on her head was obviously not naturally red when I asked.

Other than hair color, she sometimes thought about cutting herself. Sometimes did cut herself. Not as much as people thought. Not for the reasons people assumed.

Didn't seem the sort of thing I'd ought say 'Wanna do some of that now?' about. Nor something I should take a default discouraging stance concerning. I'd noted how irked she'd sounded when mentioning the general populace's tendency toward judging without all the facts.

We lingered around, waiting for my mom.

Me mute.

She talking to a buddy.

I remember it occurring to me how there'd likely never been rational reason for us to've said we liked each other or to've ever interacted to begin with.

Even more, I remember the potency of the surging desire to waste my loot on her. Drag her skimpy arm to a nearby jewelry franchise in order to insist a bracelet onto its wrist.

Or I could burn all the cash I had on me.

Set it to flame there, right before her grey eyes.

Was that a character trait which might bring more zip to our liaison?

It seemed there was no way to end the encounter *fiscally* empty-handed. So I settled for *generally*.

I set the date down in the ledger as a low-fi disaster.

Took pains to avoid the girl, thereafter.

Not difficult. Her basecoat may've been the only one in existence shier than mine.

Word in the halls was she still carried a torch for me. But I was too busy being labeled a treacherous cur by a friend who was gaga for the gal to pay such rumors any mind.

I didn't much see what my seeing her once, atrociously, and then not seeing her again had to do with her not seeing this friend, ever. Felt bound to say so.

I shouldn't have indulged her love for me, he explained.

I'd done my best not to by doing so, the way I saw it.

But if it helped, I apologized for not taking his feelings into account.

Hands were shook. All made better.

This friend was one of three I had in Art class.

Of the others, one was a fellow who'd been saddened when I'd stopped wearing my trench coat. He'd quite liked having a coat-comrade in me. Was baffled by my turning against mine.

I didn't like his coat either. Though kept it to myself. Neither garment had been of the drapey, lightweight quality from movies and television.

He'd truly committed to the look. His sense-of-self tied up in it. Considered himself wrongfully stereotyped as a dangerous loner, up to no good. All on account of some vicious acts by obviously deranged individuals our same age who'd made horrific national headlines while dressed similar.

He thought I'd stopped wearing my coat because of certain perceived social pressures he'd daily endure.

Couldn't he simply say to any detractors how he wanted to look like a Federal Agent investigating unexplained phenomena?

He'd not perform to please his oppressors. Plus, kinda did want the vampire loner vibe.

Why shouldn't he?

I felt for his plight.

The third friend was a guy I'd subject to relentless Socratic peltings on a wide range of subjects. He was a hoot because he'd never in his life addressed a single controversial idea for himself. I'd pluck the most shopworn moral conundrum from the shelf and to him it was as though hearing Zarathustra first spake.

These freewheeling, lopsided symposiums of mine didn't ingratiate me to the Art teacher. But I already had that lout down for a philistine harboring some personal grudge against me.

We'd come at loggerheads over a collage project, early on, when in a listless bit of last-minute inspiration I'd spray-cemented a five-dollar bill onto my work.

This was unacceptable.

Poppycock. Best money I'd ever spent.

It was a statement.

That cash had been given me for lunch, didn't she see?

The collage represented the nature of the struggling artist.

Physical nourishment versus spiritual.

Financial solvency or artistic legacy.

I was cautioned how in actual fact my action was defacement of Federal property. A criminal offense.

I made mincemeat of this demonstrably false claim.

Fine then. If I was going to be mule-headed, the teacher admitted the heart of the beast lay in how I was being offensive to the faith of my fellow students.

For a minute, I was intrigued.

Whatever could it mean?

Look there. Where I'd used an ink pen to change *In God We Trust* to *In Dog We Trust*.

This was belittling. A raspberry to all who took the Lord's name to heart.

Wait up. I'd no beef with religion. I thought it was neat, now that I was hearing about it all the time.

In this case, however, any ruffled feathers were unwarranted.
God in Heaven was neither here-nor-there.
I'd actually changed the motto on the bill to *In Bog We Trust*.
An Anthony Burgess reference. As I'd no doubt the teacher was worldly enough to recognize.
Such frivolous altercations.
A new one for every day.
A different me for every one.

I HAD A CLAIRVOYANCE. Could intuit the presence and location of my older brother's illicit magazines and VHS tapes. Not a single wrong guess. Ever. To this day I'll swear to my accuracy.

I'd not snoop because I wanted smut for myself. The *Mystery-Suspense* section of the Video Rental Store was more than enough to satiate what paltry appetites I had for titillation.

No. It was as though by hidden signal I'd get possessed of an insatiable hunch. Compelled to scratch the investigatory itch.

In the closet beneath the staircase leading from main floor to basement, I discovered a tranche of mags. I'd known to go to tiptoes, reach up around the bulb of the heating vent. Preternaturally.

Nearly a dozen items. In various states of disrepair. Maybe one magazine pristine, as though recently obtained. The others well thumbed. Pages loose at staples, sometimes dangling almost free. Every other item had no cover.

I'd seldom be certain when my brother might return, so my perusals were cursory and tense-necked.

I behaved gingerly with whatever I leafed through.

Additional tearing might give the game away.

Was diligent to replace the things stacked in the order I'd found them.

The pile mustn't feel different to an inspecting touch after my browse than it had before.

But one issue of *Cheri* I couldn't resist absconding with.

It contained a sequence featuring two women.
*Jasmine and Jordan.*
Everything about the images was an intoxicant. Down to how neither participant removed their socks.
Ankle-fit orange for *Jordan*.
For *Jasmine*, thick fuzzy green.
I hid the bauble inside the display box for a computer-game called *Quest For Glory III*. Dropped this behind my bedside dresser. Let various junk litter down over it so if someone scrounged around their efforts would be immediately noticeable.
Though I'd no idea what that'd matter.
To me, the mag contained what any discerning sort would've considered the jewel of the collection. Thus I'd assumed my brother made mecca to it regularly.
I couldn't fathom how it wouldn't be hunted for.
Yet it seemed it never was.
From the clear blue sky I was convinced my brother must've had some sultry movies hidden, too.
His VHS tapes were arranged in rows by his television and VCR. Many were the flicks I'd once-upon-a-time swiped from the Drugstore.
Sure enough, I uncovered a *Video Centerfold Collection*. The production featured various models, among them a television starlet much coveted by the general population.
I watched it.
A few times.
Always careful afterward to rewind, fast-forward to the exact timestamp the VCR had displayed at the start.
At first I was nonplussed.
Then bored.
Then distinctly unaroused.
The thing didn't enchant me a jot.
Too slickly produced. Antiseptic.

The lithe posing of the women seemed without narrative. Purpose. Connection to anything tangible. The sequences' overly glamorized style turned them generic. The meticulous absence of blemish, asymmetry, quirk made the women's sensuality fusty. Enhanced by make-up, lighting, surgery, the bodies left me cold.

Watching them was watching scarecrows get autopsied.

Then there was a re-recordable videocassette. No apparent difference between it and any of the ones we'd use to tape episodes of *Star Trek: Next Generation*.

Except it had crusted milk on its face.

At some point, a glass must've rested on it. Some dribbles not wiped away.

I figured my brother had left this accidental distinction in place on purpose. Tape would blend into the crowd but be quickly retrievable whenever there came need.

Here was genuine, video pornography.

Recorded from pay-Cable.

These weren't stories of erotic intrigue like what I'd rent from the Video Shop. No mid-list actors simulating passionate throes whilst tastefully filmed under soft light at suggestive but overall unrevealing angles.

These were people having sex.

What minuscule frame-story might be present likely seemed nuisance to the works' target audience.

None of the female performers resembled the alien species on the centerfold tape. Nor did they seem concerned with maintaining facades like the models in magazine spreads. No pin-up quality, fantasy elegance.

I'd no doubt a good many viewers would find them unappealing if encountered in life. Unwanted specificity. Bodies replete with too much reality to be venerated.

If they weren't there for the exact reason they were there they'd be nowhere.

The male performers seemed positively goofy. Mullets or crew-cuts. Pubic-hair moustaches. Unchiseled jaws. Even when fit, their physiques didn't make them photogenic. Their musculature seeming held on by a belt. One ham-sandwich from crumbling. They exuded fatigue. Tired of who, of what they were. The sweat on their brows spoke of effort. Stagnation.

They seemed men almost contagiously unenviable.

This cocktail of inputs, transgressive and piteous, was enough to beguile me utterly. But what made the tape a treasure was how despite the sex being clearly actual its most explicit aspects were cropped out.

No image of vaginal penetration.

If mouth were to genital of either gender the image-in-action terminated at eye-line or bridge of the nose.

Even rather creative poses were slapped with a veneer of semi-prudishness.

I surmised that allowances must've been made to air on whichever station.

Artificial zooms to the finished product.

Pan-and-scan rejiggering, after the fact.

My shepherding into the nuances of carnality was so orderly I often marvel in remembrance. Impossibly like a storybook might proceed. The world arranging matters so there'd be a gradation to what each thieved artifact revealed to me.

I think back on the mountains of material Alain and I grifted.

As though fit for a child's consumption, the lot. A kind of sterility, despite all.

Nudity. Male. Female. In duo. Trio. Quarto. En masse.

Posed as something-like-sex. As what one who knew no better would assume sex resembled.

Then the magazines hidden by my brother.

I can yet taste my utter breathlessness the first time seeing a woman's tongue lolling upward another woman's clitoris.

Will never forget my transfixed fascination with two photographed fingers buried unflinchingly to mid-knuckle.

Thinking back, I re-experience the feverishness of my mind comparing every difference between the expressions on these faces actually being pleasured to those faces I'd seen in the past. Have it re-dawn on me what a playact those first thousand visages of rapture had been.

Then videos of bodies-in-motion.

Artificial centerfolds. Meant for thoughtless consumption. For gawk. Anatomy revealed head-to-toe, but somehow excruciating.

Less clever than the fakery of a discount-bin thriller.

Hop-skip to films of the full pornographic shebang but as though peeped through a keyhole.

Humanity without hubris, but edited slant.

Secrets kept, still.

A feeling of voyeurism preserved.

I was there. Witness. But oughtn't be.

The one element conspicuously still undepicted was ejaculation.

Interesting its waiting in the wings seeing as my personal fiddling hadn't brought forth this reaction from me.

Yet.

The fateful day that happened went precisely like this.

There was a television in the cluttered dining room. Used to be in the living room, but some punitive circumstance had relocated it.

House to myself, I flipped channels.

Then I pressed *Play* to see which tape was in the VCR.

Holy mother of God …

Somewhat juddering, I gaped.

The pornography was the same genus as that on the milk-stained cassette but with no filtering whatsoever.

Shaky finger hovered near the *Stop* button.

It wasn't that I didn't want to watch.

It was a question of why I was able to.

The tape must've belonged to my older brother.

How could he have been so careless?

Instinct took over.

I pressed *Stop*. *Rewind*. Located where I'd started watching.

I needed to leave no trace I'd seen the video.

Protect it from being found accidentally by mom, dad, younger brothers.

The tape was unlabeled. No apparent identifier. I'd have to mark it some clever way to re-find. Permanent scratch or dot-of-ink. Nothing which'd be conspicuous to my brother.

But what ho?

On the cassette's lower edge, the trick was already done.

A little piece of red tape.

I felt I was in some kooky time-loop. Re-living this discovery with no knowledge it was my fiftieth time.

That thought in mind, the kitchen telephone rang.

Absolutely no reason I should answer, I nonetheless soon had my brother's voice in my ear.

Could I do him a weird favor?

'Sure.'

Was there a tape in dining room VCR?

Playing it cool I walked over, phone-cord exactly long enough to accompany.

'Uh ... yep. There's a tape.'

I wasn't to watch it, but could I take it downstairs for him?

'Should I check it's the right one?'

Naw. If it wasn't, no harm no foul.

Golly. Simple favor then. My pleasure to help.

Knowing I still had time to myself, figured I'd give the tape a deeper survey.

What exactly was it I'd stumbled into?

The sight of bodies entwining.
Clogging each other.
Faces contorting in unselfconscious galumphs.
Then something I'd never before observed.
A curly-haired man, nude except tube socks, yoinked himself free from the woman spread beneath him. His ropey semen striped the frizzy jet-black of her pubic hair. Emblazoned the jazzy brush above her spread labia in a veiny zigzag.
Mesmeric.
I ceased watching the tape.
Rewound it to start point.
Left it downstairs on my brother's VCR.
Within twenty minutes I'd re-enacted the final witnessed moment. Post-hypnotic. The deed done to myself headlong and automatic.
My depleted body felt pulpy and carbonated.
Tense as though from fright or assault.
My groin whined as though splintered.
I stared at the ceiling. Hiccoughing. Teeth chattering.
I remember figuring it was too dangerous an activity to replicate.
Never wanting to feel such sensation, again.
Wondering how soon I'd be able.

TWO YEARS PRIOR, A YEAR, even eight months, a complete stranger coming up to me with the question 'You're the guy really into porno, right?' would've sent me into a tailspin of noiac angst. So non-sequitur a query expressed in so familiar a manner. Exactly when I fit the description. The existential bends would've been crippling.
By the time the words were pronounced at me?
Possessed of a full knowledge of the world's aims on my peace of mind?

I didn't bat an eye before replying.

'Dunno if I'm that into it, my own self, but I can getcha some.'

What to make of this fellow student?

Two classes my better, he seeks me out to tell me he'd been hipped by another student I was the go-to-guy.

What, indeed, to make of his introducing himself on account of this other student allegedly having said I'd supplied them with some dirty films, for cheap?

I'd done nothing of the sort. Hadn't mentioned porn in the slightest capacity on school grounds.

My guess?

Some other student was a liar.

Or some other-other student peddled smut and now I'd got delightfully mixed up in affairs.

Par-for-the-course, either way.

Irrelevant, too.

Now having claimed I was the supplier, I'd found something to figure out how to do. Couldn't fail to live up to this random reputation.

Not even for a moment did I sound for conspiracy. Didn't entertain beyond a dismissive sniff how there might be a student on premises who knew Alain or knew some kid who knew Alain or else knew some other kid from my middle-school and thus had heard tell whichever gnarled perversions whirled around my good name in such circles.

For all I cared, that'd be swell.

I could be whatever, whoever anyone thought I was.

Anytime.

Turn on a dime.

It was simple: I could be everyone.

It's who I was.

The task-at-hand was a delightful identity.

Finagling the VCRs was the trickiest part of the endeavor.

Certain what I had in mind could be done, I nevertheless had zero practical experience in it. Knowing it ought be elementary to achieve my desired result made the difficulty I had with it entertaining. Hardly wrapped my head around the science behind plugging in one VCR, let alone where to put which *input* wire, which *output* of two of the contraptions mounted atop each other.

I seemed incapable of being methodical.

Kept no notes.

More-or-less randomly plugged this into this into that into this.

Hitting buttons.

Wondering every time what'd happen.

Even when I got the VCR configuration correct, I was never certain I'd know how to replicate it. Success seemed the whimsy of a universe which arbitrarily granted things one moment, denied those exact things the next.

This tumbling along aspect of my undertaking was glorious.

I'd not want to become too much the *technician*.

Remain the perpetual *dilettante*.

Better: I wanted it to be like I *was* and *wasn't* the person doing whatever I did. Simultaneous.

Preparing the contraband was more in my typical wheelhouse.

Reckoned I could've re-used some recordable videocassettes I had around, then decided against this tactic on principle.

Seemed like a jinx.

Classless, too.

My punters should be given top-shelf hootch.

Only the freshest ingredients used by this bootlegger.

So I'd shoplifted packs of blank VHS tapes.

Then decided I'd do my clients the courtesy of delivering their goodies pre-disguised. Save them from having to trouble their amateur heads how to keep the nasties hid from prying parents and such.

To facilitate this, I snatched some mainstream flicks. Carefully removed the labels from the tapes with patience and razorblade. Applied them to the blank tapes with brushable adhesive. The dubbed videocassettes were then slipped into the hep display boxes of whichever milquetoast actioner.

Artworks.

It was sometimes difficult to part with them.

But such efforts let my patrons know I had their backs.

Helped grow my myth.

To that end, I'd also refuse to accept payment.

'He's been at this a long time' it'd be whispered. 'A Yojimbo. Operates for reasons his own.'

Two of the most popular kids in the school commissioned me once word of my craftsmanship reached them. One even supplied me two dirty features they wanted copies of for a pal. A boon to my operation. I'd started to feel shabby for only ever having three selections on offer.

The dubbing took place in real-time.

Fifty-five minute *Centerfold* video took fifty-five minutes to copy.

I'd have the VCRs chugging along upstairs, in the dark of my parents' room, once my mom had left for an overnight shift, my dad out on whichever errands.

Limited periods of time in which to work.

Anxious my activities remain unknown in the household.

Seemed pretty obvious my older brother would guess which tapes I meant to copy if he knew I was brainstorming how to copy tapes.

Why'd I assume he'd take issue?

Why so positive he'd be upset to discover I knew of his predilections?

Because I was a romantic.

I knew his secrets but, more fundamentally, I knew the sacredness of secrets. If one had the goods on another, it behooved one to be discrete. There was a privilege in knowing something about someone else they'd deemed off limits. A duty of care.

Close calls, more than once.

My brother arrived home unexpectedly.

Heard him thump to his basement room.

The absence of his VCR would certainly be conspicuous.

But he'd either had other things on his mind and hadn't noticed it gone or else had noticed but figured maybe it'd been taken away as a punishment he'd hear about later.

Another time, he happened upon me. Red-handed.

I'd have been nicked good-and-proper if he'd pressed me to turn the television screen on. Seen the humping and bumping of mullet-man in full swing.

I'd improvised how I was copying movies for kids at school. Selling them for low low prices. Would have his machine back to him as soon as I was done.

The display box of a Brandon Lee, Dolph Lundgren extravagnza was on hand so I'd used it as evidence.

Immediately regretted it.

That flick was well known for some lurid scenes, so my brother was quick to deduce what I was trading in.

Martial arts action didn't seem the kick high-schoolers would need black-market copies of.

But a roomful of bare bosoms and a scene of a nude woman being utilized as a sushi table?

Oh, yeah. He got the gist of my little jute mill.

I copped to as much.

Which put me thinking how I might actually be able to make a name for myself, generally, without the additional risk of being branded a degenerate. At the same time, build my cover story in case one of my clients turned States.

Plausible deniability was the name of the game.

Caught with *porno*?

*I* gave it to them?

'No sir, no ma'am. I'm being scapegoated. I merely supply legitimate major motion pictures to those who can't otherwise find access. Ask these forty character witnesses. They'll vouch they've received nothing more subversive than *Quigley Down Under*. They'll tell you I've asked nothing in return.'

As many versions of myself as possible was what the doctor ordered.

Mythos and innuendo allowing me an easy out if and when I got bored of the enterprise, too.

'Sorry guys. Operations are curtailed. Some ratfink spoiled everyone's good thing by getting themselves caught and grassing me. Fret not. I've burned my Client List.'

Let people supply their own narratives to my life.

It's what happened, either way.

In this undertaking as in general existence.

Take when costume dress had been permitted for a Spirit Day.

I'd shown up in sports-bra stuffed with dress socks. Skirt of acceptable uniform length.

A teacher well-liked by me ushered me aside for a heart-to-heart. Hoped I wouldn't be scandalized, but cautioned me of the rumors going around. A substantive portion of my classmates thought I was bent.

'Yes sir, I've heard.'

Teacher didn't think so, personally. Figured I was just shy. Also, I was to understand he wasn't advising me to 'find some girl and jump on her bones.' Only to consider being observed putting a little effort into socializing. Attend dances and the like.

Told him I'd appreciated his concerns. Could see my occasional regalia probably freaked out the squares.

He surmised maybe I got more attention from girls, in the long run. A curio. Put them at ease. Told me that was clever. So long as I made my real-self known.

Our chat ended with him asking could he give a honk to one of the socks.

'That's why they're there, sir.'

He squeezed my left tit one-two-three.

Motioned to some approaching students to join in on the laugh.

Same thing with the videos, in my opinion.

Wading through suppositions for facts was nothing I'd imagine authority figures would care to waste valuable time at.

Worst case?

I was a changeling bit of gossip in the upper floor Teacher's Lounge.

I was a pornographer?

A bootlegger?

Giving things away to curry favor?

Selling to finance a pot habit or comic collection?

I was all of it, ladies and gentleman.

Choose your own adventure.

NOW-AND-AGAIN, WHO HUNG round with whom amongst the assorted common friends in the neighborhood shifted. For about a month, the dial rested on my being in the constant company of a fellow generally considered my older brother's best friend.

We got on well. A typical mix of innocence and the inexcusable. Lounged in his basement. Watched movies. Told off color, insensitive jokes.

My deductive talents revealed it was this friend's house where the dirtier films I'd dubbed copies of had originated.

Being of wealth, his household sported fancier televisions than the common scrap at mine. Remote controls summoned a menu of the endless channels on offer.

A random glimpse whilst he checked the air time for *Space Ghost: Coast to Coast* made my nostrils twitch.

Purple menu blocks labeled *Adult*.

Mint green blocks, too.

Figured one color represented *uncensored*, other color *pan-and-scanned*.

What good did that do me?

Long before the terminus of the school year, I'd shuttered my video copying service.

It'd been as long since I'd much bothered snooping my brother's stuff. His mag collection had gained a few blossoms. I'd uncovered a video hidden inside a decorative wicker basket. A flick a tad too hardcore I'd felt comfortable duplicating it for anyone.

Before summer arrived, I'd primarily focused on the distribution of mainstream cinema. Little obstacles flummoxing me to delight.

Certain VHS tapes wouldn't dub cleanly.

Originals built with copy-protections.

Sometimes only sound would transfer.

Sometimes the picture would randomly fade in-and-out, making viewing unpalatable.

I'd been left with egg on my face more than once due to these nasty safeguards.

By the time of bumming around in my pal's basement, I'd little practical need for fresh pornography.

Yet new knowledge had to be acted upon.

Such was the way of all progress.

Only those disinterested in evolving could turn blind eye to discovery.

I'd absolutely no desire to make it known to this friend I'd got wise to what was available on his TV.

It wasn't that I'd imagined he'd find it distasteful if I'd asked to watch some. Cast me out. No. Just the furthest thing from my mind was casually viewing smutty pictures with a buddy.

It'd be like with Alain.

Except all parties would possess matured physiological imperatives.

No thanks.

But this kid had more stuff recorded.

Oh yes. I could swear it.

Next to his television were four rows of VHS tapes.

Mostly proper films in proper packaging.

Several unmarked cassettes, though.

With boxes. Without.

Self-evident one of the blanks had illicit viewing on it.

Might be something hidden in one of the legit boxes, too.

Though I didn't get that feeling.

A tricky business.

I seldom had the room to myself. Only when my friend hopped upstairs to fetch delivery pizza. Even the toilet was too close to my targets. Any rummaging around while my friend was in there would be overheard.

Scant chance of distinct labels indicating a tape was smut.

I'd have to pop each into the machine.

Hit *Play*.

Scope what was what.

Hit *Eject*.

Return tape to shelf.

In antsy windows of forty-five seconds, tops.

Plus, this lad seemed sharp enough to've front-loaded the tapes with innocuous programming. Keep them rewound. Just in case.

Other plan was to swipe one VHS at-a-time.

Examine the contents at home.

Return them.

Which was ludicrous on so many levels I considered it a last resort.

To chance the zillion pointless ways the operation could be

compromised by muleing likely worthless tapes back-and-forth was plain bonkers.

The risks of being caught looking through tapes, on premises, could be mitigated, at least.

It was nervous work. Sniping peeks at the videocassettes whenever possible.

I suspected the ones with handwritten labels were the goodies.

Just as much, figured those might be red-herrings.

The tape with *Funny Farm* scribbled on the label, indeed, had *Funny Farm* playing when I'd checked.

The label claimed several other films were on the tape, though.

Which fit with my suspected security measures.

No real way to know for certain within my constraints.

I'd wagered myself an eaten hat the tape labeled *Deez Nutz Donks* was my guy.

Nope.

Home-video footage of my friend, my brother, various others shooting hoops.

Eventually I hit pay-dirt.

But matters seemed doomed to explode in my face.

My friend had been beckoned upstairs by his mother. She'd sounded upset. I'd figured I'd have a few minutes easy while he was dressed down.

Tape goes in.

Holy cats, there it was.

That same instant, I hear my friend mouth off petulant and begin thudding down the stairs.

I'd only in the nick-of-time hit *Stop*.

I had to go.

'Go?'

His mother was being a turd, he explained.

'Aha.'

The tape was still in the machine.

What was my best play, here?
I beseeched him to argue his case.
Was communication impossible?
Couldn't he apologize?
I could tell by his face this notion was a non-starter.
Sweet luck, his mother demanded him back upstairs.
I winked yeah-yeah I'd better go.
Let me take a powder first, eh?
Ducked to the toilet before being told *yea* or *nay*.
My friend remained downstairs despite a repeated summons.
I hissed internal behind the bathroom door.
Another bellow for him.
'Fine' he shouted. Jasper was using the toilet. He'd been trying to be polite. Geez.
I figured Fate had chosen to smile on me.
What finer circumstances under which to whisk the naughty tape away?
Made a beeline for the VCR.
Tucked tape to my waistband.
Saw myself out.
By now, I'd maneuvered life to have a VCR all my own in my bedroom.
Set to examining my prize, in depth.
Unlike anything I'd seen previous.
Two films. Right up my aesthetic alley.
Grainy film-stock.
Seemed shot circa middle nineteen-seventies.
No pomp or pretension. No solicitousness to what was depicted. I wasn't even aroused, despite my ungodly fascination with the unadorned look of the women.
Or was. Aroused.
Very.
Just not *crassly*.

It didn't seem what I was watching was meant to be *used*.

Instead, there was something in it to ponder. Understand. It spoke to me in a voice I puzzled to qualify.

I didn't view the totality of either feature.

During my fast-forward survey, I'd stop on scenes not sexual as often as those carnal. Hang on every overdubbed word the women said. Their every quiet. Note meticulously their expressions. Postures.

Tried to coil myself around their inclinings.

Wanted mine to be the mind inside their actions.

These films seemed naturalistic. Un-self-conscious. No overt posing or placement of camera gaze to accentuate or conceal any feature. Somehow the lens understood the simplicity of displaying these activities was its only requirement.

One film was something of a noir. The other a period piece concerning a woman's increasingly taboo awakenings while kept on the estate of some archduke.

So curious how such fictive narratives didn't dilute the verite. To the contrary. The fact the worlds these women dwelt in were ones no one really did made me feel closer to them.

I got the fear the hounds would be out to find this tape, pronto.

Vowed I'd copy it, my first opportunity.

Get it back to its rightful house.

In my cluttered closet was a green dresser I'd no practical use for. The top drawer a mess of stale cheese curls in addition to being stuffed to capacity with random bric-a-brac.

I tucked the videocassette there.

Snugged it so far back I was hardly able to fish it out.

The last place even I'd think to look if looking.

Next day was spent occupied in trivial business.

Hardly gave the tape a thought.

That night, I'd no urge to watch the films. But recall urgently stopping short in my room. Like I'd noticed something.

Though to this day I can't think of a thing I might've noticed.

I checked the drawer.

The sensation of not *fearing* but of *knowing* the lay of the cheese curls wasn't proper is as intense when writing of it now as it was in the moment. I hadn't arranged them specially. Yet I *knew* they weren't how they'd been.

I knew.

The tape was gone.

I dragged everything out of the drawer.

Yanked the drawers from the dresser.

Removed the dresser from the closet.

Gone.

No shock. This development fit.

My friend would've noticed the videocassette missing, of course. I'd be the first, best, only suspect.

My vision screwed kaleidoscope trying to reckon how the devil the tape had been found, though.

Absolutely nothing in the room looked ransacked.

I methodically examined every single place it would've been sensible to've started an investigation before landing on the green dresser.

Not one paper, one layer of dust seemed to've been molested.

Yet my senses weren't out to sea. I'd noticed the cheese curls. Felt their wrongness on sight.

I didn't understand.

Not that it mattered.

No negative interactions with my friend transpired over the subsequent days. In fact, we were yucking it up per usual.

When I checked his shelves, the recently stolen flick wasn't present. I'd know it by a chink I'd made in its casing.

This tracked. He'd be more cautious with it now.

Yet something didn't sit right.

Next day, I crept to my brother's room.

Right there in his row of tapes I spotted the identifier I'd carved.
Popped tape to VCR to confirm.
There she was.
Yep. There I was.
The videocassette remained in my brother's possession a few weeks.
I neither copied it nor watched it again.
One day, it was gone.
I've no idea was it returned.
Imagine it must've been.
Under which circumstances?
I'll never know.
The wheel had spun.
Dial landed different. Who hung round where.
The world another new version of its same self.

.2.

I COULD ASSURE MY DAD. No. I wasn't a devil worshipper.

It was three-in-the-morning. Seems the school had contacted him several days prior. Before the weekend. Explained various accusations which'd been leveled against me.

He must've figured it best to've waited until the wee hours to clue me in. Right before I was to return to class.

It was all news to me, certainly.

To his credit, my old man wasn't one to believe the hype. The way he saw it, I'd probably been engaged in a literary debate. Referenced the works of Thomas Mann. Goethe.

If not?

He suggested I go with that line.

I would've preferred him to think the claims baseless. But good to know he'd been working on my out.

I figured he was kooky. Had misconstrued something. Until I was getting off the bus and the hayseed driver motioned me over. Told me in confidence he didn't believe I went in for anything like what was being whispered of.

He'd gone to bat for me.

Told them they were barking up the wrong tree.

Turned out it was some innocuous triviality which'd snowballed.

Some freshman kid's mother had overheard him repeating inappropriate jokes I'd told.

To save his skin, he'd laid it on thick.

I'd cornered him.

Him and others.

Compelled them to listen.

Wielded my influence as a sophomore.

For good measure, he'd claimed I'd curried his general favor by giving him cash money, unprompted. Which explained why he'd been able to afford some things his mother had wondered how he'd acquired.

The woman, somewhat a zealot, had put the two to the two and the four was I was Satan.

I couldn't deny being a gregarious guy. Affable. Quick to share a buck.

Despite whichever subjective opinion on my comedy stylings, these were all fine traits.

Didn't the administrators interrogating me admit as much?

But this was another in a long line of incendiary happenings I'd been at the heart of. It was getting tough for them to allow for benefit-of-the-doubt.

Speaking of jokes and blasphemy, had I forgotten the controversy surrounding my election speech?

The one which'd begun 'Who'd win a fight, me or God?' and was punchlined 'Me ... because there's no such thing as God.'

Not to mention whooping the senior class into a frenzy by removing my uniform sweater, hurling it skyward whilst screaming 'Freedom'.

I'd already explained. The joke had been deployed to rivet my audience. Get them in my palm. Like Cicero might do. Not to mention I'd no way of knowing how, mere days previous to my speech, the seniors had lost their privilege to dress in uniform, minus sweaters.

Pure coincidence my theatrics had been interpreted as specific political propaganda.

Plus: of course I remembered the controversy.

They'd made me shave my head afterward.

I was still carrying my hair around in this plastic bag, wasn't I?

It was once more pointed out how earnestly they frowned upon my doing that.

Well, there's nothing in the Handbook restricting me from carrying a non-transparent bag.

'Your fellow students know exactly what's in that bag, Jasper. What it means.'

Of course. They'd seen it on my head. Semi-baldness or a bag in my hand had the exact same effect.

Reminded my peers of the consequences for actions like mine, right?

They simply had two ways of interpreting it, now.

I knew they'd heard skeevy chatter about me being some low-rent pornographer, too. Situations unconnected to my previous year's endeavors kept such rumors under their microscope.

I'd become one teacher's go-to-guy for recommending which films would be neat to show in class on free days. Never suggested anything askance, but when he'd inquired if *Altered States* was suitable to show in Physical Science I'd giving the thumbs up.

Had I forgotten about the torrid sex scene and graphic dialogue harkening back to it?

Honestly?

Kinda.

But who'd believe that?

The teacher affected by the minor fiasco considered the mishap a hoot.

Among the student body, the oral history of the day had taken on a life of its own.

Legend became I'd bamboozled the teacher into screening the film in order to show off my reach.

Descriptions of the sequence-in-question grew absurd.

Then there was the complaint about my drawing the Lord Christ's penis. A totally drummed up charge. I'd doodled the crucifixion. Period.

'In yours, Our Savior was butt naked.'

As we'd been discussing in World Religions that exact day. An entire lecture expounding differing accounts of *Golgotha*.

Where had the nails been driven in?

Palms?

Wrists?

Was Jesus robed, in loin cloth, bare bottomed?

Varying depictions of the miracle littered the historical world. Right up through popular culture. We'd in the same week been shown the film *Jesus of Montreal*, for Heaven's sake.

'That movie doesn't depict the gonads.'

Doesn't mean they weren't there.

Added to which, I drew my sketch on the back of a vocabulary quiz. Wasn't exactly cramming anything down people's throats.

They were correct. Yes. It so happened I did have an answer for everything.

I'd buy magic beans if ever offered some, too.

When had that become a fault?

As to the bogus allegations of enticing fellow student's into compromising their morals through participation in games of chance?

I maintained my longstanding position.

Since my randomly doling cash out to my classmates was met with clutched pearls, I'd found a venue to part with it sportingly.

I'd never *gambled* with anyone. I'd *lost money to them*. On purpose. For my own kicks. I didn't even know the rules to any card games let alone how to score-keep dice.

I certainly did carry around gambling paraphernalia.

What did that have to do with the price of tea in China?

It was my passionate stance there were certain perfect objects in this word.

A deck of playing cards.

A regulation pair of dice.

Just as there were perfect sounds.

A well-executed bridge shuffle.

The clatter of craps about to be shot.

Denying this was a fool's errand. Might as well disown billiards chalk, a cork free of wine neck, the *thwit-t-t-t-t* of a rotary phone, or the crumble of gravel under tread of reversing tire.

Yes yes. I was quite the everyday poet.

But they'd had enough of my verbose recalcitrance. Their point had been made, regardless of my need to posture.

Next, I was given the brass-tacks of my situation.

Shape up. Or be forbidden access to the bus.

I'd still be responsible for getting to class. If I missed too much class, I'd be expelled. Tuition wouldn't be refunded.

Did I want to waste my parents' time and hard earned money?

'Not everything is about you, Jasper.'

'I hope so' I wanted to say.

Instead, I nodded.

Mute.

Was dismissed.

The rest of the day piddled by.

People slipping surreptitious stares my direction.

Others demanding I regale them with what'd transpired in the bawdiest way I might.

One friend took me aside for a private word in the library corner. Somberly asked me to consider that maybe I'd taken things too far.

'I literally didn't do anything, man. The charge was *devil worship*. You know?'

He supposed I was right.

I could tell he only *supposed*.

By the time I climbed back onto the bus, the entire situation felt like something I'd heard someone sing once. Lyrics I was now able to put context to.

I could see myself the villain. Or at least the rascal.

Fair was fair.

If someone genuinely believed the devil could galvanize as an entity who interacted in a common way with the physical world, I might seem like him. His agent provocateur.

That made sense.

Quite a headspace. Coming to believe me to be something like that.

But the belief was based on this mother's beliefs.

As well as her belief in her son.

As well as her belief he shared her beliefs.

Nothing in this mother thinking me some ghoulie was at all unreasonable.

If I was one, it's not like I'd think I was.

Added to which, I was jealous of her.

Believing I was a distillation of the supernatural, mingling with the anonymous denizens of a tiny school to tempt the young to damnation via recycled jokes and two-dollar poker?

Really *believing* that?

Magnitude and minutia, at once. Each containing the other.

Spectacular.

I couldn't mock it. Didn't try.

I had all manner of inventions in my head no one's point-of-view could disabuse me of. Certainly not with pat observations or sophistic gainsaying.

I only saw life in abstracto. So had taken it for granted the way religious thinking worked was as half-make-believe.

That inclination wasn't anything I'd originated.

Its reality nothing I'd verified.

Just something I'd seen.

Nabbed up.

Considered mine.

Really believing *anything*?

It was difficult to fathom.

Take the events of that very morning.

I'd understood everything my interlocutors had said to me. Snaked from that understanding even as I'd inwardly accepted it.

While I cogitated on these existential mud puddles, one of my fellow bus-riders sheepishly took the seat across the aisle from mine.

Leaned in.

Copped to being the cause for the day's events.

It would've been bad trouble for him like I'd no idea if he hadn't run me off a cliff. He'd never meant for his mother to get calling around to other mothers, though.

I wasn't mad at him, was I?

We were still friends?

Of course I wasn't mad.

Why wouldn't we be friends?

He told me he was sorry.

'You've nothing in the world to apologize for. That's why I'm here.'


THROUGH A FRIEND CALLED DAMON I secured part-time work at a six-screen, strip-mall cinema. Same one where I'd had my first date.

Changing from school uniform into the rudimentary outfit of employment in the establishment's restroom is among the happiest I recall ever feeling. Could've existed in the intermission between being one thing and another forever.

Stared at my reflection.

Posed and adjusted my nametag.

Adjusted my nametag and posed.

The cubby box of the joint's lobby was a wonderland. Stale carpet, trod past flat except for violent warbles to random lengths. Perpetual mustiness, part mop water, part popcorn steam, part pretzel cheese, part wafts of my own perspiration risen by a perpetual loiter of humidity due to overset heating. A sharp blur glazed the lenses of my glasses from asinine neon proclaiming *Tickets, Snacks, Auditoriums* or else striping the walls arbitrarily. Reflections of posters on each other's glass display windows, smears of light off tiles peppered odd colors none of which seemed their colors correct. Constant *bw-rawk* from videogame units and Skill Crane, slush of a machine breaking patrons' bills for quarters while they clattered joysticks, punched buttons, chattering vowelless and incomprehensible.

Often my senses pulsed, overwhelmed. Unable to keep from focusing on all the world at once.

It felt like I worked buried under wet laundry at the base of my skull.

Nothing could've been better.

Tidying up auditoriums was Heaven.

Squinting in pulpy almost-pitch-dark after the last patrons exited. Running push-broom dust-bin device over dapples of popcorn, candies. Bagging trash the discourteous didn't bother finding receptacle for.

Ensconced in music swollen with impotent bombast as the rolling credits of films I only knew from interchangeable letters of entrance marquees yawned in peripheral vision.

There was an occult serenity in taking a seat, center of back row.

Alone.

Music.

Names I'd never remember affixed to job titles I didn't know the meanings of clinging to their association with films I'd never seen.

Perfect contentedness.

Relaxing in what felt precisely like after The End.

My mind giggled with methods to pickpocket fortunes out of the job. The monetary aspect, of course, being incidental. Cash had mostly evidentiary value. Quantifiable proof of the cleverness of a scheme.

Considering I worked alongside a friend, every grift seemed that much the easier to pull off.

Imagine if we rigged things so it'd be the two of us plus another pal working together. Another. Another. Comrades in perfect cahoots. Running our own business hid smack in the guts of the business employing us.

'It'd be like getting paid for two jobs working one' I pitched to Damon.

'Or like running the risk of losing a steady job and bringing down criminal charges which might ruin future prospects' Damon Socratesed back.

Under the conditions I'd outlined?

We'd never be at hazard.

Didn't Damon understand?

Then let me explain.

We'd memorize the prices of common items, what change to be dispensed from whichever denomination tendered.

Press cash register buttons like normal.

Pop drawer, but leave transactions unfinalized.

Delete what'd been entered.

Everything'd look kosher from the patron's point-of-view.

With no co-worker to worry about, the thefts'd be silken.

'Say they want a receipt?'

Hardly anyone cared about those.

Besides, we'd wait until last-minute to erase the orders. If some film buff suddenly needed a paper trail, it'd be a simple playact of 'Let me reprint that for you.' Finish the transaction legit.

'We do inventory, man. If sales rung don't match cups and bags in stock it'd be red-flagged. Just like they know when candy is missing.'

Check out these popcorn bags we toss out while bussing emptied theaters. Some of them hardly touched. If emptied, given a spit shine, a second use wouldn't be noticed. Same with most cups. We'd clean them out, obviously. New ice, new drink, new lid, new straw.

What difference to a moviegoer?

We'd agree between us how many bags, cups per shift to resell.

A steady number.

A regulated intake of extra funds.

Inventory would tally.

We'd be a well-oiled machine.

Not a whiff of impropriety to us.

Yes, I understood it wasn't the most sanitary hoodwink.

What was ever 'the most' anything?

'We're talkin' *Department of Health*, possible legal action against the corporation, if one thing you might've never anticipated goes wrong, Jasper. For what? Extra five bucks a week? Work an extra shift, man. Heck, work an extra half-hour.'

Was everything always about money with Damon?

Final offer.

We were legitimately allotted free popcorn and drinks each shift.

True or false?

So could we spin that straw into gold, at least?

The monies had already been tallied into the company ledgers.

We were just performing some alchemy.

Didn't he feel we ought be able to ask for cash value over sugar water and junk food?

Wasn't it us being stolen from if we didn't partake?

The company pocketing a quick buck off our discipline and good health?

No. Damon didn't see it that way. Sorry. He just didn't.

Added to which, he'd probably use the money to buy a drink. Or a popcorn. So considering he already had access to unlimited he'd be shorting himself.

It was moot. I realized it even before his silly retort.

For the free drinks, we were required to utilize the tiny cups specific to employees. Different bags for the popcorn.

Did nobody but me see how romantic the world wanted to be?

How constraints, definitions tented in the boundless experience its wilderness wanted to afford us?

Certainly my boss didn't. Blinked at me cross-eyed when I'd refused to simply apologize for giving away free concessions to customers.

Splitting hairs, I'd pointed out it wasn't *free concessions*.

I'd let certain people have Large beverages instead of Medium. Same with popcorns. Only sometimes and only ever when they hadn't wanted to spring the extra quarter I'd diligently tried to glad-hand them into forking over.

Sometimes I'd upped them from Small to Large, sure.

One time I'd bought candy for a kid out of my own pocket.

Maybe that's where he was mixed up.

That act had been in service of proving a larger point, however.

A parent wouldn't get something for his daughter because he'd said it was overpriced. If it was free, I'd inferred, he'd gladly have lavished her with what she'd desired. The outrageous mark-up and not his own heart was keeping harmony from a family outing.

My gesture had confused the man, in the moment.

In the end?

I'm certain he'd thought back on the experience fondly.

None of that equaled giving anything away for *free*.

Money went *into* the till.

*Every* time.

Granting my points tentatively, the boss regretted I'd made what I'd done out to be fouler than he'd been aware.

Didn't I think actions such as I'd described might give unreasonable expectations to customers?

Make them think all cashiers would pay their way so long as they pled some unique case?

A tacit promise given from the establishment through one of its ambassadors?

I could hardly account for some theoretical member of the general public being certifiably insane.

What if someone came up and claimed that'd happened without my having confessed it?

We'd not believe them.

In this case?

We'd know they'd be telling the truth. But they'd be asking for more free stuff after having been extended extraordinary kindness.

Hardly the sturdiest moral legs they'd be standing on.

Oh the boss understood. Was right with me. Comprehended all my other points, too.

Most people don't eat all their popcorn, anyway.

What real difference in cost to the company, buying bags this size or that?

All a shell-game.

Robbing Peter to pay Paul.

Yes, he'd been working Movie Theaters for decades. Nothing new under the sun, my fine observations included.

'But your *job* is to ask for those extra quarters, Jasper. Someone doesn't want to pay them? Fine and dandy. Thank them kindly. Smile. Someone doesn't eat all their food? Drink their full drink? That's their inalienable right. But we give them only what they *pay* for. That doesn't make us *thieves*. Quite the opposite. The deal is: we're free to ask them to pay what we want, they're free to decide whether they want to pay it. They're free to come here or not for any reason, logical or illogical. It may sound harsh, but it wouldn't be untrue to say I don't care about the people, personally. I care about their *patronage*. That's the job I've been given to work. To care about *that*. You have to decide if you want to work the job *you've* been given. The one you freely *applied* for. The one you say you *enjoy*. You're not required to. You can stand outside. Give people money for tickets and candy to your heart's content. But not as an *employee*. That's kinda the deal. It's why you have the job you have. To *do* that job. We're not thieves for doing our work. Nor can we be thieves while performing it. Doesn't that seem fair?'

It seemed uncannily fair.

I could fall in love with the equity in his speech.

I told him I understood.

Then thanked him sincerely for the past three beautiful weeks.

MY FIRST KISS WAS A stage kiss. So I always say. In preparation for my role in *Plaza Suite*. Script called for it. Scene partner and I both paused. Confirmed with the teacher we were supposed to actually lock lips.

'That's what it says.'

It was. We did.

In the play, I'd enacted a lothario. The choreography for the make-out with my co-star was intricate. Thorough.

On the night of the performance, we'd agreed I'd up the ante. Risk the parents in attendance rushing the stage to lop off my hand.

My hand which'd slithered under her dress.

Two fingertips tracing the center of panties I can still feel the scalding cotton of.

Standing ovation.

My myth grew in buckets.

The teacher who'd advised me to apply myself socially so as to dispel churlish rumors tousled my hair. Called me 'You dog you.'

My actual first kiss was also a stage kiss. In its way. Earlier that year. With a young man I'd met outside of school. We'd simply kissed. I suppose because we'd wanted to. Removed as it was from any other aspect of my life, the midnight parking lot had resembled a rehearsal stage.

That kiss I never included in my story about that young man. A sprawling tale of hitchhike and crazy circumstances over Christmas break. Greatly embellished. That genuine aspect elided.

There'd been hitchhike. A little.

Even the hopping on-and-off a slow moving freight-train was true.

Everything else in a gargantuan letter I'd penned to the girl my third first kiss would be with was spun from whole cloth.

That third first kiss was my real first kiss.

We'd decided that.

Yvette and I.

The ones for the play hadn't counted.

She'd no idea about the other. Though was aware I'd previously wanted to kiss boys.

Though this, in itself, wasn't true.

Not exactly.

Regardless. In the sanctioned history, Yvette was first.

I'd kissed a dab of brownie batter off her nose. Then later, our lips met in the ordinary first time fashion. Shy and overemphasized.

Yvette was my sweetheart, good and proper. Reciprocally, I'd turned adolescent cartwheels in the role of hers.

When Candy-Grams were being sold, dollar-a-pop, in service of financing prom I'd purchased fifty. Had them delivered to her during Math class. All in a pile. Unique, handwritten notes from me in each one.

She'd never want to end our nightly telephone calls. I'd tell her 'Go to sleep, then. I'll keep talking.'

Then would.

No understanding of long-distance charges, I'd built expenses in the hundreds-of-dollars. When my parents informed me and enacted limited talk-time, I'd taken to not returning home after school.

Remaining in Yvette's town.

All night out of doors.

Or in bad weather in Post Office lobbies.

Quarters for pay telephones. Local calls. Unrestricted.

Yvette had refused to watch me in *Plaza Suite*. But heard play-by-play ad nauseam, after the fact.

Her jealously intrigued me.

Tame but still bristling.

A wonderful curio.

I was paly and flirty with everyone. Part-and-parcel to my vow of always acting ten times more confident than I was.

One girl, Pauline, was an especially sore spot for Yvette. Formerly her dear friend.

Beautiful girl, Pauline. Gave off the simultaneous impression she'd be voted Employee of the Year at three separate soup kitchens and Most-likely-to-be-Lolita.

Pauline had sighed during lunch how no one had ever once given her flowers. I stole three silk roses from a Crafts Store. Presented them to her, next day. She'd stammered. Then hugged me like a mouse trap.

Pauline had sighed in Science class how glum she was over her forthcoming birthday. No longer *Sweet Little Sixteen*. Would need a new theme song. Nobody else smart enough to, I'd belted out the opening lines of *Saw Her Standing There*. She'd blushed atomic. *The Beatles* were her favorite.

Rumoring eyes covered these occasion like frostbite.

I got where Yvette was coming from.

Her jealousy was understood.

She didn't want me fantasizing about other girls.

Especially in *that* way.

I promised her I didn't.

Not mentioning I didn't fantasize about her, either.

In *that* way.

In that way I fantasized *as* her.

In matters of reverie, it'd always been my penchant to embed myself in the skin and mind of the female. Since purloined nudie mags, videos viewed, up through reliving times spent with Yvette or cobbling imaginary ones.

Even in thoughts of that boy I'd kissed it'd be me cloaked a girl.

Or else he'd be a girl.

But I'd be him.

I understood my desires best as someone else's.

The candid confessions of female classmates about boys or each other had always been more kin to my unconscious currents than any from male classmates toward anything.

Erotic letters allegedly penned by women set me afire.

Not only with urges toward self-pleasure.

But toward pontification.

Was I *like* that which they wanted?
Or did I *want* that which they wanted?
Did I want to *be-them-wanting-it*?
I'd think back to the *Plaza Suite* performance.
Relive it as though feeling someone's hand on my actress thigh.
Fingers resting on fabric outside me.
Didn't want that hand inside me.
Wanted my own hand.
Inside the *inside* I wanted.

But lacking that requisite, my exterior sufficed more than pleasantly.

I'd no inclination to not be myself. Especially not with Yvette. But decided being one's self didn't mean blathering one's every last crumb, willy-nilly.

Nor acting on every desire.

Something Yvette, herself, more than knew.

Though keen to initiate certain kinky fun, personal beliefs kept her from proceeding to intercourse. Despite equally personal desire to do exactly that.

She'd confessed to me she'd confess to the priest in the box every Sunday about our various jaunts. Appreciate the absolution.

She'd struggle with explicating her confusion over this earnest attempt to balance who she was with who she wanted to be. Would apologize for the confessions as though needing absolution from me.

But what to repent?
No one was really anyone.
Or better say: no one was anyone yet.
I thought this all so very profound. In those days.
How *yet* was perpetual.
Never exactly *now*.
*Now* was not *yet*.

*Not yet* was *now*.

It could well turn out to be true that no one'd ever be who they were. Or who they wanted to be.

I felt zero pull toward repentance.

Why wring hands over your genuine or counterfeit self?

What difference between performance and unwitting reveal?

The audience, only.

Their astuteness.

Their aptitude to interpret what's there. To understand you without having you spelled out in alphabet soup and spoon fed them.

At school, I'd speak in farcically poor accents. For days on end. Well past good friends begging me to knock it off.

For several weeks I'd acted in imitation of a favorite television detective who'd, on the show, suffered a stroke.

Genuine concern from my peers. My teachers.

Why was I moving so slowly?

Having trouble finding words?

I'd explained I'd suffered a fit of nervosa.

When I'd got bored with the game said I'd been successfully treated.

After, I'd pulled some muscle which'd resulted in my arm involuntarily twitching. So claimed the tic further result of my condition.

Did nothing to treat the actual injury so that the phony ailment might endure.

Told Yvette I took pills procured from a doctor I'd gone to without my parent's knowing.

Would pretend to swallow these in the company of people.

But never let anyone see them.

As with the overblown tales of my hitchhiking exploits, Yvette took these confabulations for the reality I claimed them.

Harmless, I'd thought.

No point disabusing her of the deceit.

Less in abusing her with the truth.

These fantasies sewn into my life were nothing to do with who I was. They *were* who I was.

But to insist on bringing such difficult-to-pin-down aspects of my fluxing mentality into a spotlight would've come across as fabricating cruel nonsense. Trying to rid myself of her. Or else pulling some dastardly switch.

'I'd made you fall in love with who isn't me. Now insist you love who is.'

Say I did that?

All versions loved Yvette back, just the same.

What difference?

I sounded it out, thusly.

She'd believed I'd been *homosexual* based on no evidence except my saying I'd been when asked.

Wasn't *relieved* when now I *wasn't*.

But wasn't *not relieved*.

I'd originated no epithet, merely accepted whichever came.

When they went away, I'd accept their replacements.

What difference?

Ought I tell her I was more interested in doing the things she wanted to do to me than I was interested in doing things to her?

Explain how, in my mind, I lived from her perspective?

Even if she understood, she'd only understand what I couldn't.

I'd be pretending to understand *as* her.

What she *understood* was what I'd *perform*.

She'd told me once she felt bad that I loved her.

Figured, at least in some way, I wanted to be with a boy.

But I didn't.

Didn't want to be a boy, even. Not really.

Nor wanted to be a girl.

Or be with one.

The proximity to someone, playing the role of what I always wasn't, brought me surfeit of pleasure.

I wanted to *want*.

Didn't matter what I was or who.

*Wanting* could be done from anywhere. As anyone.

She worried she'd changed me.

'You haven't' I'd told her.

Hadn't told her 'Because there's nothing to.'

YOU MIGHT FIND YOURSELF IN the company of someone. The both of you coatless. Short-sleeved. Yourself in cloth shoes. Struggling through an expanse of thigh-high dead weeds, winter sharp. Might realize your conversation has morphed to legitimate assumptions you'd both soon be dead from exposure.

This might be all on account of you'd taken a half-witted wrong turn on the way from a pal's house to the Supermarket. Your joint aim having been to shoplift rolls of film.

When such a thing happens, if it does, it'll be safe to assume you've found a best friend. Soulmate. Twin-brother.

Before such mid-winter near-death, chances are you'd have already met. The bond such hours of severity would make indelible will have been introduced.

A million inexplicable times.

Days before you'd have spotted a well to-do house in the six-am distance.

Weeks prior to your maybe-last-breaths.

Months before chattering monosyllabic decision to go knock on the door, beg yourselves inside to thaw.

An autumn in advance of such defining moment, exactly who it was you'd been expiring with will have been made abundantly clear.

Or so my experience would indicate.

Nathanial had found me. Freshman year. One day handed me a compact-disc he reckoned I'd enjoy.

I'd said 'Thanks' or thereabouts.

Put the thing in my backpack.

Not thought of it again until the night before the last day of class. Found it, case cracked, at the bottom of the bag where it'd been left. The self-titled debut of *They Might Be Giants*.

I often remark the providence in it all. How the thought hadn't crossed my mind 'I'll just keep this.'

Instead?

Concern for propriety.

I'd best listen to some of it.

In case he asked me about an opinion.

So I'd popped the disc in the player on the floor near my bed.

Laid down.

Pressed *Play*.

Those first two beats. *Dant dant*. The most exquisite sounds I'd ever heard.

Through sophomore year we'd become attached. I recall no standard introductions. No moments of questionnaire chit chat.

Not a single memory, either, of wondering should we bother.

We had, in essence, already happened.

Any idea he had gloved the hand of any idea mine.

Any frivolity I suggested was a pick unneeded to a latch he'd already turned.

We'd often have read the same comics. If we hadn't, sought out what the other one referenced. Likewise with films. Television. Whatever was shared with the other was treasured for the gesture. Made immediate, permanent fixture of reference. Regardless our opinions on whatever it was.

Nathaniel struck me as a Jasper who hadn't committed to imposture. The kid was all the things I was but which I'd chosen to make myself seem anything but.

A performer devoid of playact.

His shyness was shy.

Humor unrehearsed.

Feelings genuine, present, unfiltered.

When a certain remark made me realize it'd been he who'd handed me the note from the girl I'd gone on that silly first date with I'd felt ashamed. He'd built, still tended quite an unrequited flame for her. I felt embarrassed for having been obstacle. Wanted to seek out the girl. Shake sense into her.

What had she been thinking, using the Real McCoy as conduit to the topaz?

Nathaniel shrugged when I told him this. It hadn't been up to me. Up to him. Or up to her, probably. Things went how things went. This had gone that way. Then had gone the way it'd gone.

Which was exactly how I saw things.

But it sounded legitimate when he said it.

As with all else between us, I learned theft would be assumed reasonable a priori.

Every situation was a code to crack, a caper to orchestrate. Whether we even cared to go through with a scheme we'd scheme one. Sit for hours after school, on weekends, ingesting *Roy Rogers* hamburgers. Gleefully outlining in pedant minutia the endless nuances of how we'd get away with theoretical chicaneries.

Or we'd steal, proper.

On principle.

For the Art of it.

From Shopping Mall chain-stores we'd smuggle novels we'd never heard of. Lift even better ones from a mile-long Used Book re-seller. Only the finest criteria utilized to select targets. Liking a title. An author's name. Design work on front cover. Fragrances to pages. Type fonts. Wear to spine.

If we stumbled upon an interesting edition of a title we'd already stolen?

We stole it, too.
If we found five distinct editions worthwhile?
We'd take them all.
We possessed divining rods.

Nine-out-of-ten volumes absconded with became our favorite works of literature. Lifeblood. Remain so to this day.

The remaining volume would without fail be something we'd revile. Such titles came to serve as shorthand for ridiculing all which shouldn't exist.

Never paid for movie tickets.

Once in the confines of an auditorium would sit through films twice if we fancied.

Theater-hop to another if the mood struck.

It'd be unacceptable for a VHS tape we wanted not to be ours.

Box had a tricky security device?

Didn't matter.

What belonged to us ought be with us.

If we were caught?

All in the game. Bitter with better.

But we never were caught.

We'd outline thefts in Kantian detail. Execute them as though murder plots from thrillers where things hadn't ended well for the killers despite any discerning viewer knowing things ought to've.

Enjoyed committing the violence of prying loose, cracking open the plastic protections of compact-discs. In the public privacy of parking lots around corners from shops out of which they'd been stole.

Slicing the bellies of merchandise boxes to scoop out the item guts. Right on the sales floor.

One of us lookout.

Other one handling the wet-work.

Nothing more beautiful than frames for prescription eyeglasses, we'd pocket the floor samples from chain Ophthalmologists.

Scratch the designer's stamp from the plastic lenses.

Or Nathaniel would wear the frames with nothing inside.

We'd concoct personas around purloined electronics. Pocket dictaphones. Microcassettes by the package. Roam school corridors between classes conducting absurdist interviews with students and staff. Invent bizarre character voices to recite impromptu rants in.

Our school chums would listen to these, rapt. Repeat them around. Turn our off-the-cuff balderdash into underground catchphrase.

Nathaniel took this game as far as clandestinely recording cuckoo dialogues with anonymous telephone dispatchers. Would grill whichever operator answered a Directory Assistance line about their favorite Renaissance thinkers.

I remember particularly well a certain afternoon.

A snatch to be undertaken.

Every chance of alarms going off.

We'd not hashed out a workaround.

Best either of us had come up with?

Wait until staff were furthest from the entrance. Parking lot empty as it got. 'We'll head out the door, keep walking, be out of sight before anyone can do anything.'

I'd been hesitant. Insisted there must exist solution more elegant. 'Some citizen might hassle us. Or what if an eager-beaver store clerk gives chase?'

Nathanial explained no passer-by had legal right to accost us.

As to store clerks?

'It's like the Headless Horseman' he'd calmly saged. '*Once you cross that bridge, my friend, the ghost is through, his power ends.* In public air, no law can touch us unless we confess.'

I've no doubt he knew this was wrong as much as I did.

But phrased the way he'd phrased it, anyone arguing what was right would be wronger still.

Poetry trumped credibility.

Adherence to it worth more than innocence.

Nathaniel understood the proper composition of the world was personal. Its parameters to be curated. Every individual's their own. All that was was what one surrounded oneself with.

Physical. Philosophical.

Horde the trinkets and baubles of reality you find kin with. In them discover the marrow of you.

He'd never stolen anything before meeting me. So his outlook was all the more spellbinding.

I thought of the wasp rattle of experiences which'd built my perceptions into what they were.

His easy embrace of the same conclusions made him seem a savant.

Yvette knew we were thieves. As well as someone who isn't a thief can know. Had the finest innate apprehension of the subject I've ever witnessed in a layman, in fact.

Understanding notwithstanding, she'd prefer we not ply our trade on premises of the part-time job she'd secured. Café attendant in the bookshop portion of a Greeting Card Store.

We understood.

Showed restraint.

However, there were titles we definitely wanted in this quaint establishment.

Some could be found elsewhere, there was no arguing that.

But no place on Earth was simpler to lift from than this cozy nook.

It'd beggar reason to take greater risk for merely the same inconsequential result.

We'd compromised by not bilking certain philosophy magazines we'd coveted. The vast wall of periodicals being the bread-and-butter of Yvette's section. Strictly inventoried. Especially the more specialized titles.

By summer, I knew Nathanial wouldn't be returning the following school year. Off to fancier education. Halls with honest-to-God ivory scribbled on them.

So any moment not with Yvette was with him.

My sleep taking place on his sofa.

When that wasn't possible, I'd spend the night on some bench near his home.

Or else I'd bum about insomniac.

Listlessly drift through closed strip-malls the hours till sun-up.

Body stiff and impoverished by the time of our next 'Hello.'

Mind on the blink.

Soul needing neither.

.3.

THE CHOREOGRAPHY OF THE SCENE was approved by faculty.

Detective, me, would enter stage-left. Approach captain, Damon, sat behind desk at stage-right.

During our initial lines, I'd fish cigarette pack from hip pocket. Slap it to cupped palm *whap-whap-whap*. Fit ciggie to lip.

Damon would, amidst his lines, casually strike a Zippo lighter. Real flame snapping crackle. Hold it my way.

'No thanks, I've quit'.

Lighter snapped shut. Damon's captain unphased.

None of this remotely to do with the mystery farce one-act.

The moment had the desired effect upon audience.

Parents gasped. Postures tightened.

The laughs of relief made clear how we owned the room.

Deal was I'd return the pack to the custody of the teacher directing.

Immediately upon leaving the stage.

To be inspected. Its contents having been thoroughly catalogued.

The pack had been full when first shown me by the teacher. Bought by her. With money I'd given.

I'd opened it during a rehearsal.

Unloaded a few sticks.

Crumbled them.

Littering fuzzy remains into a waste bin while giving detailed explanation why it made sense my former smoker would carry a half-empty pack.

I'd left two smokes unbroken in the mess I'd discarded.

In an opportune moment fished them from the receptacle.

One for Damon. One for me.

My recollection is hazy whether Damon smoked his. I seem to think so. In my presence. But it may've been he'd gifted it to a mutual pal who'd sucked the thing down.

I'd kept mine hidden at home. Where I seldom was. Secreted it in the same computer-game box containing *Jasmine and Jordan*. Would take it out, time-to-time. Draw its tight length slowly in brushstroke under my nostrils.

Delectable staleness.

My mouth watered the way it did at black licorice.

Nights not spent at home, I was derelict in the town where my school and Yvette were.

Quite often I'd crash at Damon's place.

Though this wasn't exactly sanctioned by his family.

I'd initially asked could I use his ratty old shed as a home-base.

For reasons of arachnophobia, we'd settled on I'd tap on his window when I required port in a storm.

Would need to be gone by first light.

Weekends, it was often permissible I be over without need for sneakiness.

Offered the sofa.

Breakfast.

General hospitality.

I felt monstrously awkward those times.

During such weekends, Damon and I would take walks past midnight. Down the wending podunk road from his house to the school.

We'd gab.

Philosophize.

Dream up movies to maybe someday make.

Roam the graveyard grounds of the campus.

Climb fire escapes to roof areas commonly off limits.

It came to pass that various construction was being done to the school gymnasium. The contractors neglected to lock up, one night.

Unable to believe such luck, Damon and I set to exploring the classrooms around the basketball court's perimeter.

Snooping through desk drawers.

Fiddling with science equipment.

Interchangeably tip-toe and singing tunes at the top-of-our-lungs.

Normally at center-court, secured to the high rafters, there hung a massive American flag.

This'd been taken down for ceiling work to be undertaken.

We came upon it in a box we opened while looking for neat equipment we might abscond with as souvenir.

Laid out full, the banner was one-of-me wide, almost two-of-me tall. The material less pleasantly tactile than I'd have guessed. Like a discount rain slicker.

It struck me as artificial.

A toy flag.

Regardless, it was irresistible.

Considering my lifestyle, it wasn't feasible for me to be the one who kept the trophy.

So it went to live with Damon.

I'd have soon forgotten all about it.

Except after a short time its absence was noted by school administration.

The only reasonable conclusion was a student had made off with the thing for a prank.

The teacher who'd taken such concern over my masculine reputation gave an impassioned plea. A man of military service, he spoke of the reverence such symbol deserved.

No investigation was to be launched. He wasn't asking anyone to turn themselves in. Though if the culprit did come forward, their identity would be kept anonymous.

Barring this, it'd be appreciated if whoever took the flag would leave it on the gymnasium bleachers.

I knew Damon still had possession of it.

One night a horrendous thundershower had lashed me while I'd been far from any reasonable shelter.

Soaked to the skin, I'd wandered floodwaters to his house.

By the time I got there, I'd been so thoroughly drenched it'd hardly seemed worth bothering with stirring him.

I'd thought to sleep beneath a tarp in the back of one of his parent's trucks. Only the thing was a veritable wading pool.

When he'd blearily let me in through the bedroom window, I observed how Damon was utilizing the flag as a blanket. I slept in some clothes he lent me beside him beneath it.

For sure he wasn't going to turn himself in. He believed there'd be no consequence. It wasn't that.

Just why lose face in the eyes of this teacher?

Agreed.

Plus, I didn't see why he should return it without mentioning me.

That said, I certainly wasn't going to fess up.

I doubted it'd be seen as anything but another incident to roll a collective administrative eye at were my confession proffered, but one never knew. The safe-passage deal offered the general student body might've contained an asterisk leading to small print disincluding Jasper from protections.

True to what the teacher had said, no inquest seemed afoot. Letter-of-the-law, his word had been kept.

But in spirit?

For weeks, every teacher made loaded remarks in class about integrity. Couldn't help letting on their disappointment the flag hadn't been returned. How disheartened it made them feel that no explanation had been given to faculty about it, in private.

Even the average student seemed bent out-of-shape to know a ratfink walked amongst them.

It bugged me, all this.

Fouled the beauty of forgive-and-forget.

Bygones bygone.

Sleeping dogs left to lie and all.

Damon decided things needed to be put right.

I wasn't so certain returning the emblem was good science considering how much time had elapsed. I made no bones how I'd no intention of letting my name be connected to the incident. Tried to nurse him around to reason.

His take?

He couldn't exactly use it as bedspread anymore, eh?

It was a miracle how only I was privy to his having done so.

By now, his parents knew of the situation. If they came across a gigantic American flag folded and squirreled away, his goose was cooked. Or if some other friend was over to hang out and espied it. They might get afflicted with an acute touch of religious morals and grass on him.

Good points.

Especially the last one.

With all the psychological tactics the faculty was up to, no telling who might've turned into a closet goodie-goodie.

He'd simply leave it anonymously, he concluded.

I was a tad chagrined.

It was mine as much as his.

Such inauspicious end hardly befit this scenario. Let's not turn our backs on romance, please and thank you.

I understood it'd be senseless to dispose of it, outright.

Besides which, the teacher's heartfelt plea had wormed its way into Damon's better angels.

It'd seem a conscious desecration of his bond with the man to chuck the flag in with the rubbish.

I could get behind that.

Maybe the teacher was onto something about the intrinsic value of symbol, too.

To that point, a plan was hatched.

The object was inspected thoroughly.

Any identifying mark whatsoever which might reveal it to be the exact flag that'd been filched?

Any conspicuous wear-and-tear which made it appear less than brand new?

Seemed not.

Did Damon have any boxes from items mail-ordered?

Preferably with generic postal label still affixed?

Good.

How about a length of plastic such as a coat might be delivered in?

Okay, close enough.

Styrofoam packing peanuts or blank crumpled newsprint, brown craft paper?

Presto.

We had ourselves the perfect prop.

None but the most cynically suspicious mind would think twice over this being a delivery from a bona fide Flag Supplier. Along with the box, a letter bearing no signature would be presented to the teacher. A gift from the entire student population.

Greatly moved by his words, astonished by the cold heart of the thief, a hush-hush petition had gone around. Whoever could kick in a buck or two to order a new flag in the exact style of the one which'd been purloined had done so.

Beauty was?

The story of the gift would get a speech, too. Everyone lauded en masse for this show of decency and self-sacrificial heart.

That no one sought credit would make the gesture seem truly a cut above.

Further?

I knew I could count on the nature of Man to make this false story real.

No one had been asked for money.

But since the note didn't say literally *everyone* had contributed, it'd make sense to hear 'I wasn't asked for anything' when students conferred amongst themselves.

Plus, such honesty reinforced how everyone was keeping humble about it.

Only the poor asker, who'd contributed nothing, would feel left out.

Given time, this person or that would claim they'd thrown in a buck. Or knew someone who had. But wouldn't name names.

A zillion impromptu white lies from the community would congeal to make the overall lie demonstrably true.

All of us in it together.

Proud. To be who we weren't.

WE'D DECIDED TO MARRY, QUITE early on. Yvette and I. Inside a month, if memory serves. Nothing else seemed sensible. A natural declension from high-school sweetheart, first loves.

Legalese required some time to pass before ceremonies were permissible, arrangements could be stamped official.

Therefore, a period of fiancée was more than reasonable.

No time like the present, I'd procured a ring. Proposed one fine day between classes.

Yvette's mother picked us up after school, most days, in order that Yvette and I could spend some hours together.

Before I'd wander off into the night.

Find a pay telephone for bedtime chats.

Then seek shelter for sleeping.

Or spend the overnight reading Supermarket paperbacks.

On occasion, I'd sleep on the benches right outside the school's primary entrance. Try to wake with enough time to hide before teachers started pulling into the lot.

Sometimes would let myself be found out. Explain I'd needed to be dropped off early by my parents, that day.

Usually be permitted inside.

Out of the cold.

Would get some shuteye, head on my crossed arms at a library table.

On the day of my proposal to Yvette, no sooner were we seated in the van than she'd showed off her bauble. Made our betrothal known.

Pulling out onto the road, Yvette's mother had assessed the situation. Dubbed it plenty adorable.

However, she'd not accept the terminology 'engagement ring'.

Insisted the modest jewel looping her daughter's left hand, fourth finger, was a 'promise ring.'

In no way was this a reflection on me.

I'd made fine impression on the family. Was in very good standing so far as that was concerned.

Indeed, it tickles me every time I think back to Yvette's introducing me to her father. How she'd reported to me afterward, quite giddily, the first thing he'd asked upon my parting had been 'So what's he *really* like?'

He'd meant my bearing, manners, style-of-speech had pleased him greatly, yet still figured it must've been the game-face which boyfriends knew to utilize when required.

She'd insisted that how I'd behaved was what I was actually like. Informed him with pride how I was the same with everyone.

True.

More than she knew it to be.

What Yvette's mother had meant was simply that we were quite young, yet.

Not that we wouldn't wind up marrying.

We were to understand this.

Her point was she saw little percentage in ordering invitations dated for the day after graduation. Would hold off contacting the clergy or even decorating the dinner table with a *Congrats* banner from *Party Mart*.

I didn't see what the big deal in this was, but Yvette had taken it to heart.

Considered the remarks churlish. Unwarranted.

Her mother was entitled to her point-of-view, same as anyone, but could've at least been courteous enough to've kept the dismissive phrasings interior. Thought meet to put an antic disposition on in order to let her daughter enjoy the endorphin high of the moment.

My natural inclination was to counsel Yvette how since she and I knew the ring signified a serious and committed engagement it ought be fine to let be.

But after some weeks had gone by during which Yvette heard the words 'promise ring' a handful more times, I came around to fully endorsing her position.

Whose side was I on, after all?

In that connection, I'd set to cobbling up money through a mixture of the usual legit and nefarious methods.

Good chunk from my dad by way of daily lunch money.

Modest thefts from his wallet.

Begging a few bucks to buy a book or two I'd claim were required for school. Then stealing said books to prove the money had gone where I'd claimed it had.

Also I'd newly discovered a skeevy Video Store which would

purchase used materials. The joint primarily trafficked in porno flicks but had a secondhand shop of mainstream offerings in its front-room for window dressing.

Didn't pay out much per VHS, not even for entire collections.

But since I'd never been out the cost of original purchases, what skin off my nose?

Soon enough, I'd bought Yvette a second ring.

Not much difference in price-point than the initial one.

But that was hardly the point.

I'd waited for a good lull in conversation to address Yvette's mother, some afternoon. All of us sat around in the living room. Told her I'd been thinking over all she'd said. Had concluded she was in the right. Her wit and sagacity appreciated.

The ring Yvette wore was a mere *promise*.

Any fool could see as much.

'However' I added, producing the svelte box from my pocket, opening it to a pleasant creak, turning toward Yvette '*this* is an engagement ring.'

I hoped any previous semantic business could be laid to rest. Provided, of course, Yvette would do me the honor of answering the question I put from bent knee in the affirmative.

This gesture altered nothing, so far as I could discern.

But Yvette appreciated me socking it to her condescending old mam.

It'd been my pleasure.

I always found it enjoyable to comport myself in a fashion which demonstrated grandiose romance was possible.

This little controversy had been a gift, quite frankly.

I made it a habit to get up to such capers whenever I could. Always looking for an angle. A way to one-up my previous bravura.

Sometimes I was aided by Fortune.

Such as when there'd been a choker for sale in a downtown

Thrift Shop. Yvette had swooned over it, but I'd already spent my last dime on hamburgers.

On the walk home, smack in the park grass, lay a plastic baggie full of cash.

I'd snatched it up.

Turned us back around toward downtown.

When Yvette asked shouldn't we wait to see if the rightful owner showed up I'd pish-poshed.

Obviously the choker was meant for her supple neck. God himself had chosen this mysterious way to prove it. Otherwise the world was pure chaos. I'd never accept that.

Other times, I'd put in some elbow grease.

In the Shopping Mall where Yvette and I hung round was the bench on which we'd loitered when first daydreaming of our getting hitched.

I'd decided *that* bench ought be hers.

In preparation for a scenario I'd dreamt up, I again set to scrimping dough together. Worked up a few words of poetic sentiment to carve into the bench's backrest. On account of how lovely Yvette always said it was when we'd see things like that on trees in the park.

Tables in diners.

Sidewalk squares.

Then I'd set to manifesting the moment.

We'd been poking through stores quite idly when, as though out of the blue, I'd stamped my foot. Announced to Yvette how the bench in question was her property. By divine right. I'd not rest until she had it for keeps. I'd been thinking long and hard about this. Enough was enough. Now was the time for action.

With all haste I brought her along to the Shopping Mall's business office.

Affecting my finest aw-shucks humility I addressed a receptionist.

'I've not made an appointment, but might I have a word with whoever is in charge of the benches?'

Without more than three minute's wait, I was granted an audience with a fellow who called the shots.

Got right down to brass-tacks.

Told Mr. Big I had such-or-such amount of cash money on hand. What was going to happen was I'd put said monies in his pocket. In exchange, he'd let me leave the premises with my marriage bench, unmolested.

He kindly asked Yvette and I to return to the reception area while he gave consideration to my proposition.

I had a Plan B on the simmer.

In my heart, rather hoped things didn't pan out, straight forward.

Drastic matters were fun to resort to.

If the deal went South, I'd call on Damon.

He had access and occasional permission to drive his parents' vehicles.

In the past, we'd stolen bags of mulch from out front of a Supermarket.

My idea. In some insomniac surge of pride, I'd declared it arrogant of the store owners to flaunt their wealth in the face of John Q. Public.

They had so much mulch they'd leave it around unprotected, eh?

Were just so cocksure no mortal would dare double-cross them?

We'd see about that.

Probably we would've taken the wicker lawn furniture left out, as well. If it hadn't been for Damon closing my hand in the truck door. My screeching the appropriate racket to accompany such wound.

So it'd be a cinch to vamoose this bench, if push came to shove.

Turned out there'd be no need.

The power-man, with some flunky in tow, approached Yvette and I. Hand extended.

The bench was ours.

With two conditions.

Firstly, they'd accept no money for it. We must consider it a gift. That was the sort of people they were, not another word on the subject.

The second condition was we not take the bench away with us, right then.

With our blessing, they intended to have a special placard commissioned. Engraved upon it would be a subtle commemoration of the Shopping Mall's part in things.

Never fear, it'd be a small, tasteful bronze plate.

Affixed to the bench front, somewhere unobtrusive.

Agreed.

Jolly good. We'd be contacted in a week to arrange pick-up.

Yvette left the encounter walking on moonbeams.

I left kinda down in the dumps.

Now the bench was a *gift*. Not purely a *result* of my efforts.

The money in my pocket ached to be frittered.

But to reveal it at this juncture would be ruinous.

Yvette was under the impression I'd bluffed the power-man. Used my charisma to render him hapless. Had made him want to impress me.

I desired to maintain such illusion.

Didn't think Yvette would find what I'd really done near as alluring.

Felt a bit lonely for that.

INSOMNIA HAD ALWAYS SEEMED LIKE a hot ticket. Look at that word. *Insomnia*.

I wanted it.

Told people I had it.

In reality, nothing could've been farther from the truth. I'd sleep for weeks if left to my flesh's weak whimsy.

As with most curio I coveted, if I wanted insomnia I'd have to take it.

Live the effect unafflicted with cause.

So I pushed myself to shun sleep.

Vagabond nights became increasingly unconcerned with finding spots for some rest.

Formless weekend afternoons when I'd no one to hang out with, I'd tended to pay for City Bus tickets. Would sit in back. Zonk out. Even though drivers got mad at me. Claimed I was abusing public transit. 'You can't buy one ticket and ride the bus all damned day.'

Now I'd avoid such situations like the plague.

No way to fend off the Sandman when lulled by seat vibration. Sonorous engine hum. Rock-a-bye of stop-start progress across town.

In my secret heart, I'd hoped to contract insomnia through impersonation. Body so accustomed to lack-of-sleep it'd begin to crave the awake. Physiology acclimating to its own deterioration.

A kind of reverse exercise.

Photonegative to athletes craving exertion, finding it harder to rest than work out.

I'd go twenty-four, forty-eight, seventy-two hours without more than a chin-fall of snoozing.

After which I'd lose a solid day to the *Zzz*s.

During this same period, a condition I genuinely suffered from began presenting itself more aggressively. In retrospect, I wonder whether mucking my circadian rhythm served as an accelerant.

Whether so or by mere coincidence, episodes of sleep paralysis became frequent. Far more lucid, disconcerting than the sporadic nightmare bursts experienced in my childhood.

These episodes simultaneously horrified and bewitched me.

Before a dream scenario took its turn for the ghastly, it'd be lushly detailed. Fully sensory. Auditory. Tactile. Olfactory.

Events seemed to transpire in real-time.

I'd consciously recollect them, moment-by-moment.

Wake with the impression I'd been fully conscious for whichever duration the slumbered narrative encompassed.

I fancied I was being gifted extra periods of waking life.

My response to this notion was cultish.

I desired means to induce the state.

Preferably without the horror-shows.

Though I'd accept those if they came.

Somehow enjoyed what the condition made me.

Different.

Haunted.

Accursed.

I became fixated on procuring periods of bonus-existence.

Attempted to mad science my way to them.

I'd taken note how night-terrors felt similar to the syrupy sleep I'd experience when medicated for flu symptoms.

Further, there was a trend in them being most vicious when I lay on my back.

Especially when passed out from exhaustion, fully clothed.

Moreover, when I'd sleep wedged into the crevice of mattress and wall, I'd often stir from oven-warm slumber unable to roust myself. Similar to the paralysis. But free of the interior screams.

I'd down quadruple doses of *Nyquil*.

Snuggle stiff under comforter.

Screw my head into the wall corner.

Mouth agape.

Even kept my shoes on.

Curious semi-sleep was produced. I vaguely recall that.

But no true memories of it have endured.

Which is completely different than with paralysis dreams.

I recollect those, chapter-and-verse. When present day instances strike, oftentimes they directly reference slumbered panics from ages ago. Every time make me re-believe there is some separate, linear continuum they grant me access to.

Regardless of the laboratory failures, I became fond of the soupy head I'd have following such experiments.

Took to treating myself to swigs of *Nyquil* recreationally.

To keep my mind grubby.

Give my perceptions something to work against.

Days became a struggle between my fervent desire to never sleep and the medicine-coursing-me's passion to put out my lights.

In this bohemian head, I determined I'd direct a stage play.

When the school wouldn't let me take the reins of the official Spring Production, I decided I'd arrange a competing show.

Schedule the same Opening Night.

We'd see who had the last laugh.

As it was something most students were familiar with, I settled on staging *The Crucible*. Reckoned the film having come out a year or two prior would make it easier to direct.

'Hear how Daniel Day-Lewis said that line? Just you say it like that, too.'

I schmoozed the folks I thought'd make the best cast.

Promised I'd handle everything.

They simply needed to work out the lines.

Contracts signed, I announced I'd have scripts to them presently.

Certainly I could've found the nearest photocopier to tend to this.

But that seemed so chintzy.

No.

Pristine editions of the play would be whisked without payment from bookstores. This was to be a class-act production. No corners cut.

I'd overestimated how many copies would be on hand at a given retailer. Even after emptying the shelves of every place I had access to I was short.

Suddenly I was struck with the brainwave to check my local library. How looting such a palace had stayed off my radar till then I remain dumbfounded by.

I wanted every *Permabound*, oddball edition in the joint.

Wanted to peel off the adhesive strips with dates stamped on them.

Remove the disused pouches for catalogue cards from back inside-covers.

Tear the triangle of every page corner.

Feed them to pigeons.

To snakes.

I'd steal the termites out of the establishment's walls, if opportunity presented.

All I made off with, though, was nine copies of the Arthur Miller.

It'd be satisfying to say the preparations for the play were a fiasco.

In reality?

They weren't even a pratfall. Just an uneventful meander toward the cast losing interest.

Not one true rehearsal ever materialized.

I blamed myself.

Wasn't cut out for leadership roles.

Sulked.

Plodded on with a minor role in the school-sanctioned theatrical.

Following a Saturday rehearsal, I waited out a downpour before setting to my medicine-head wandering.

Everyone else was long gone.

Except for a flamboyant lad called Pierre. Bull Goose Looney of the Drama scene.

He seemed concerned how I'd no way to get home.

Told him my parents were running late. No worries.

Man of conscience, he couldn't abide leaving me in a lurch.

I oughta come have a seat in his nearby car.

I'd not've noticed him locking the doors if not for him pointing out 'I have to lock the doors. They pop open. Weird car.'

Nervy from knowing no ride was coming, too bleary to come up with a clever curtain line, I blathered. Got to grousing over my directorial debut's failure.

Pierre's face went buttery empathetic.

I shouldn't take it so hard.

Would've put on a terrific show.

He knew it.

Said it was a shame he and I didn't get together more.

People like us should always help each other out.

I was shrugging 'I guess' when he moved to seal his open mouth over mine.

I squirmed an indication we weren't on the same page.

'Oh come on.' He turned out lower lip, petulant. 'Don't be such a girl.' Nudged my knee with his. 'Lemme cheer you up.'

I removed his hand from my arm. My head a muddy boot-print filling with pond water.

He winced. Insulted. 'What's you deal, man?'

No deal.

Just waiting on my ride.

I'd wait outside if he'd unlock the door.

'Why are you being shy? Are you worried people might find out about it?'

I remember mumbling 'About what?'

In my mind the inflection had been a snort.

He must've considered it foreplay. Next moment, no blush, had leaned back and said 'Dunno ... a little blowjob?' His legs spread. One knee jammed by steering consol. Other raised while he adjusted his seat's recline.

So dejected, his sigh as he growled his frown like some kindergartner before unlocking my door.

Such disdain, his huff as he closed the zip of his pant-front.

Without eye-contact he muttered 'I don't get you, man. But, yeah. Go. Be whatever.'

No longer in much mood to stray around under foul weather, I used the pay telephone outside the gym to call my dad.

Waited the usual hour for him to arrive.

I'd sit. Nodding off.

Stand. Throwing punches.

Recite various things I could've said to Pierre while I did both.

Skipped out on classes for a few days, after.

Spent the days stomping around my old hometown haunts.

The Comic Shop hadn't changed. Welcomed me with the scent of cardboard, brown bags, newsprint grade paper.

The proprietors took up gabbing as though no beat had been skipped since last I'd been in.

In the course of our banter, I got round to the raucous tale of my attempt at theatrical fame. Worked to relate it as grandiloquently as I could. But had to truncate it unexpectedly when I got to the bit about not having scripts.

One of the proprietors laughed during my preamble, saying I should've tried the library.

Without thinking, I'd blurted 'That was my brilliant streak. Figured, while I'm at it, why *borrow* them? *Stole* them instead.'

They both made cartoon *tut-tut* faces. Waved me off like I'd told a joke in bad taste.

Flustered, I stammered, nodding I-know-I-know-I-know as I clumsily backpedaled.

'I'm saying wouldn't that be funny? If someone did that.'
Funny?

They seemed reluctant to go so far. At best admitted they could see it being humorous 'in a story about some *scumbag*.'

Finally noting I'd got sheepish, the more gregarious proprietor relented. Motioned me please-go-on.

Having known me since I was yea-high, he promised me he got what I'd meant.

'*Jasper* stealing? From a *library*? That *would* be funny.'

To imagine me the sort of crumb who'd ever sink so low.


I COULDN'T HAVE STOPPED MYSELF slipping baby Jesus into my pant pocket, gun to my head.

There the tyke was.

Amongst the manger scene cast-of-characters.

Mary.

Wise men.

Animals seeming duly impressed.

An absolutely generic figurine. Holy the way only a factory stamped mold could be.

No. Nothing could've stopped me. It was all I could do to keep myself stealing the miniature troth the babe slept in.

Except he wasn't sleeping.

Our newborn Lord gazed right up at my fingers moving toward him. Eyes would've been wide and innocent when his face smooshed into the closing scoop of my shadowed palm.

This theft was executed in the presence of several witnesses.

A yoink on the way down the steps from Philosophy class before lunch.

I don't recall whether I'd remarked the diorama, any time previous. Set in the recessed nook at the turn of the stairwell, halfway down.

Whether peripherally aware of it or no, the impulse to snatch had been unconscious.

Thoughtless.

For a laugh.

Which'd been had.

By all.

The Christ was fashioned from a substance similar to the balls vended for dimes from crank-turn devices at the fronts of Supermarkets. Those ones which could 'bounce to the moon.'

Except Christ wasn't bouncy.

More like one of the collectable monsters I'd played with in childhood. Those *Muscle Things* formed of pink industrial gum.

Thinking back on the figurine in particular, it makes sense I'd taken it.

As a kid, it would've intoxicated me.

Been the exact sort of trifle I'd see on display and daydream about.

Feel subatomic connection with.

An imperative to possess.

But in the moment?

No real desire, at all.

None specific.

I'd absorbed it the way an amoeba might've some bit of dead protozoan.

A stimuli response.

Borne of a nature which was innate.

After it was mine, I hardly gave it second thought. Didn't take it out to preen over. The thing simply kept to the pocket of my khaki uniform pants. Quite forgotten.

Not surprising at all, therefore, what came next.

Not at the time.

A retroactive shock, though.

Whenever dwelt upon in these decades subsequent.

Why had I done it?

Why had it felt I'd done nothing?

In Gym class we met out-of-doors. To run laps around the soccer field.

Me and my cadre of cronies weren't ones for exertion, however. I'd stopped even changing my clothes. We lot merely strolled. Shot the breeze. The teacher sensible enough not to care.

As we skirted the tree-line to the dense woodland flanking the school, I quite out-from-nowhere unburied the Christ from my pocket.

Displayed it a moment.

Delicate pinch between forefinger and thumb.

Said something to the effect of 'Betcha didn't know Our Lord and Savior could do this, didja?'

Wound up.

Took three power-building strides.

Zipped my arm in an overhead haymaker.

Flung the tiny object into the wilds as far as I could.

This drew a communal guffaw. Lasting all of ten seconds.

Then the group fell back in step.

Continued our banter as though never interrupted.

Life went on as always it had.

No reason, of course, that it wouldn't.

At Morning Assembly, weeks later, the Headmaster took to the podium special. The day's general business sorted, there was some matter only a dignitary of his relevance could address.

In funerary tone, he explained how one of the women who worked in the cafeteria, a humble personage whose service to the school was long standing, had lost an object quite precious to her.

The Christ from the manger scene which'd dwelt in her family since time immemorial.

He was sure we all knew it.

The one on display in the main building's stairwell.

She was heartbroken.
Pleaded through him for its return.
His own plea ratified hers.
Please. Return this cherished property.

The Headmaster enunciated his own anguish in knowing a student could be this callous. To've made off with such an Icon. Criminality aside, he simply couldn't fathom what anyone would want with so personal a belonging.

An object which could mean nothing to them but obviously would mean the world to its rightful owner.

That said, he needed to be clear in expressing how he wasn't imploring the matter be rectified for his own sake.

Nor was he speaking on his own behalf, at all.

Indeed, all gathered ought understand that, possessing a heart so kind as she did, the lunch-lady had vouchsafed a guarantee from him there'd be no punitive measures enacted. Well the woman understood the sometimes unmannerly whims of young boys and girls who, for reasons mercurial, get up to mischiefs all manner.

No need the culprit suffer public unmasking. She asked only the Christ be returned.

The final word from the Headmaster was to explicitly state that if whoever had taken the figure would simply lay it back to the manger the matter would never be breathed of again.

I was sat in a row with the friends who'd witnessed my purloining the doodad. As well as with those who'd laughed when I'd hurled it directionless into the woods.

Their eyes met mine.

Widened.

I shrugged.

There was nothing to be done for it. I told them as much.

Gee whiz, were such a feat possible I'd gladly give the thing back. I quite liked the lunch-lady. As guileless a soul as could be encountered under Heaven. Beautiful as a spent teabag. To be appreciated as fondly for all the sweetness she'd imbued.

From time-to-time, I'd fancy I heard whispers among students on the stairs.

*Nobody'd returned it?*

*Unbelievable.*

No way anything could be proven, I nonetheless prepared for what I'd say if one of my pals turned canary.

I might be dinged to pay a fine, I supposed.

It'd been made clear the manger scene was no longer in production. Discount bin trinket when originally purchased now primly and valuably vintage, no doubt.

Though such was hardly the point.

That'd been laid out plain.

The thing gone was priceless. Irreplaceable.

Nothing merely *resembling* the object could satisfy.

Wouldn't have been touched by the same hands, breathed the same living room air as however many children, grandchildren.

So on.

Soon enough, the matter would fade.

From my mind.

From everyplace.

My name need never be associated.

Those affected got the picture.

Something had happened to this miniature Christ.

Whether carelessly misplaced or heartlessly consigned to the underbrush it amounted to the same.

Such was the way of all flesh.

It wasn't as though I had information on where to find the remains in a Cold Case and was keeping shtum.

I put it out of my thoughts.

Until.

Again at Assembly, one morning.

Damon made his way to my side.

Announcements were still being given, so I returned his nod, nothing more.

A few minutes passed.

He nudged me.

Held up a tri-folded leaf of paper.

I gave a paly wink like I knew what it was though hadn't the foggiest.

Noted the serious cast to his expression.

The anticipatory tilt to his posture.

On the paper was a handwritten confession. Quite heartfelt. Damon taking the rap for the stolen figurine.

He wrote how it'd been some stupid impulse. Childish. Stated he'd lost the thing over the course of carrying it around. Had searched. In vain. Couldn't ever apologize enough for the harm. The fact he'd had no comprehension of the deep connection it'd had to the lunch-lady was no excuse for his action. Regretted sincerely how all he had to offer her was his sincere regret.

In truth, after gleaning the gist of the document I hadn't bothered with too close a read.

Turned to Damon. Whose eyes awaited response.

I may've wrinkled my nose to mean 'What're you doing?'

Though may not've.

Was I meant to co-sign?

Did he fancy this a favor being done me?

I was bewildered.

What could prompt an innocent man to throw himself under the bus in this fashion?

Did he feel guilty he'd been bystander to my deed?

Was such vague culpability a weight on him?

At best, I could see such business drawing a private frown, now-and-again.

But this?

Entirely foreign behavior to me.

Somewhat daffy.

Damon taking the heat wasn't only nothing I'd ever ask of anyone, it was an act in aid of diddle.

Did he think it'd help the lunch-lady?

With what?

Maintaining her faith in the basic goodness of the students at the school where she toiled?

Preposterous.

If she'd kept even half-an-ear open she'd have heard plenty to warrant a pause. Just in the three years I'd been on site. That's even barring all rumors about me. There'd been a fair share of scandals. From plagiarism to drug-use to an affair between some basketball player and an Art teacher.

This was a place. Same as anywhere.

We were people. Same as anyone.

Or did Damon get some peculiar kick doing this?

Was there pleasure in false confession?

The act some private delicacy?

He tapped forehead toward me. Eyes puppy-dog.

What did I think of the letter?

I returned him a smirk. Cockeyed.

Was he being serious?

Then passed the paper across.

He nodded.

Impenetrable.

To this day, I've never asked him a thing about what happened next.

.4.

I'D JUMPED OUT THE WINDOW during English class. First sitting in the open frame. Then draping one leg over sill lip. Other leg following so that my back faced the room.

Let myself drop.

I'd gauged it wasn't too high. Chance of broken limbs, sure. But no limb broke.

Had landed with an awkward bounce and stumble.

Ambled around the rear of the gymnasium building.

Re-entered the classroom.

Teacher had *blink-blink-blinked* but not questioned me about where I'd been or when exactly I'd left.

Apparently she hadn't noticed a thing.

Hardly anyone had.

The few students who'd watched me jump hadn't thought it worth reporting, I supposed.

That was early in the week. But the event kept on my mind. Remained front-and-center come the weekend.

There was something to it. Though I didn't quite reckon what.

Did people pay so little attention to me?

Had I achieved utter anonymity?

Or perhaps everyone did pay attention. But I'd become mere observable phenomena.

A flicker on a screen.

Did this.

Or this.

Or that.

No interaction warranted.

None possible.

Was I a storyline to reflect on but to never confuse with something which might be altered?

I'd defaulted my interpretation of the aftermath of the jump to 'man, that's funny.' At first. Then got wondering what would've happened had things taken a bad turn. Had my action been recognized. Interpreted. Responded to.

A million things. Maybe.

Not that imagining them mattered.

Nothing had happened.

No one felt any one way or another.

I felt whichever.

Everything remained moot.

Such considerations doodled in my mind while I plodded along. Walking my bicycle. Bicycle which'd been Nathaniel's idea to start using. Toward the end of the summer.

Imagine the distances we could cover with ease.

The exertions spared us compared to tromping all over.

I'd not been able to stand riding the thing.

Still couldn't.

My nerves weren't steely enough for such a contraption. The bagginess of the kung-fu style pants I wore had the garment's cuffs constantly getting snagged in the spokes. I downright mistrusted my physical ability to negotiate curbs.

But still these months later I'd not arranged for a place to leave the vehicle off, permanent.

Loading it into the car when my dad ferried me to my hometown wasn't worth the headache.

Couldn't dump it at Yvette's because her mother was under the impression I rode it to where I'd meet my parents, each night.

Lord knows why I hadn't simply abandoned it on the side of some road.

Or pawned it.

This exact morning, I was considering doing precisely that.

Would be nice to have a fist of sudden money.

Gift my gal with some surprise.

Far too early to knock on her door, I decided to wait out the hours until meeting Yvette on the bleachers of a baseball field nearby her house.

Bike was leaned to the backstop.

Trusty old manual camera and rolls of film rested on the corrugated metal where I sat.

My appearance was lowdown. Ratty cloth shoes held together with duct tape, rubber bands. Hair a long, unkempt rat's nest of uncombable matts, dyed red. Face of a gaunt cartoon pauper. The hang of my shirt made it clear the body beneath had committed to heroin chic.

Not at all astonishing how my lengthy presence had raised alarm in the hep community surrounding me.

A policeman exiting his cruiser explained from afar he'd been summoned to sort what-from-what.

'I'm just waiting to see my girlfriend.'

Didn't seem this passed the smell test.

Was that my bike?

It was.

I could prove that?

Didn't suppose so. No more than I could prove my shirt belonged to me. 'Did you have something in mind?'

Yes sir, he did. Positioned his uniformed body to block my view of the two-wheeler.

Was there a serial number on it I could tell him?

If there was I'd never seen it. If I'd seen it, certainly wouldn't have it committed to memory.

What kind of bike was it?

Really didn't know. A mountain bike of some make. 'Is there a report of a theft in the area?'

He merely thought it interesting I knew so little about my own transportation.

'I'm not an avid cyclist.'

Looked a bit small for me, too.

Did I see what he was driving at?

I laughed. He was spot on. No doubt would make detective soon enough. One of the umpteen reasons I hated riding the bugger. Thing'd been mine since I was a kid. Was way too big for it, yeah.

This conversation was getting to be a real hoot. Accused of stealing my own bike. What a delicious development. I'd have to insist the screenwriter include it in the eventual major motion picture of me.

The cop'd got bored with that game, though.

Was on to asking about the camera. That was mine too, he supposed. Though bet my bottom dollar I couldn't tell him which brand it was.

'Got me dead-bang, officer.'

Go beat that, eh?

What's in those little canisters lined up on the bleacher beside me?

'The film containers? To judge by their likely apt name, I'll hazard a guess they contain film.'

So I wanted to try out my cute bits on him, did I?

Maybe I'd better stand up. Leave the camera. Step over there.

Not exactly true, but told him I was happy to comply while I did.

Mind if he opened them up?

Couldn't think why I ought to.

Interesting.

Wasn't worried it'd ruin the film?

As I couldn't picture him unspooling the things, exposing them to direct sunlight ... no, no I wasn't.

So he was going to find *film* in the containers when he looked?

'Out of curiosity, what else did you think you might find?'

Considering I wasn't worried, why do I ask?

It was absolutely just *film*, after all.

I concurred with him there. Pointed out I had said 'out of curiosity.'

He gave inspection. Nodded privately. Took a beat. Asked if I had other rolls on me.

'Other than the one in the camera, no.'

Okay wiseacre. I knew what he meant.

What's inside my pockets?

Good question.

My guess was just the inside of my pockets, but it'd been awhile since I'd checked.

I don't have a wallet?

Sure didn't. Kept my money in my shoe. Not that it was his business.

What else did I keep in my shoes?

'My feet' I said like spoiling a dim first-grader's attempt at a riddle.

Take them off. The shoes. Keep the feet where he could see them. Well, well. Thought I'd said I had money down there.

'When I have money, I do. Times are tight. Haven't you heard?'

Turn out my pockets. Fine.

Now turn around. He was going to pat me down.

Apparently my physicality struck him as above board.

But, by the way, what was my name?

Here I knew our rapport was about to hit a snag. Hoped my simply going 'Jasper' would suffice.

'Jasper what?'

Couldn't I catch a break? Why'd he need to know my name?

'You don't wanna tell me your name?'

Oh I was dying to tell him my name.

'Jasper what?'

Jasper Escolanzo-Mirabal.

There was the look I'd come to know and love. Those narrowing eyes. Those lips pursing tight. Gorge risen halfway while measured breath puffed out a flaring nose.

'What's your name, son?'

But my name genuinely was Jasper Escolanzo-Mirabal, he ought rest assured. I was aware, to the untrained eye, I looked to be named anything but. My dad's fault. The man hailed from a foreign land. Though not from the one the officer was probably supposing. Folks there were world-renown for their pallor and deep, stentorian voices.

'Show me your identification.'

Made croupier gesture of hands-empty. Indicated my shoes, over there. My already turned out pockets.

'You don't carry identification? What about School ID?'

School didn't issue ident cards.

Which wouldn't have mattered, he explained. Still giving me the glare. Those could look like anything. Easy to fake.

I was glad I didn't have one, then. That sure woulda been suspect what with my also sitting around in a legally permissible way with my own camera and bike on hand while wearing shoes and having been named something.

'You all done with the lip, son?'

I was, officer. Beg pardon.

What had happened, he'd have me know, was an elderly woman had taken fright from my hanging round.

Loitering for a suspiciously long while, according to her.
Seemed to have been yammering to myself, all the while.
Last straw was she'd seen me stretch out for a little lie down.
Which isn't against the rules of the Public Park. No. Though were one a pedant, the technical hours for sanctioned community activities didn't begin until ten.
Factor into it how the bike had seemed little.
See what he meant?
It may also interest me to learn that those who traffic in illegal drugs were jolly fond of using film cans to hold nuggets of marijuana.
Add it all up?
Reasonable assumption was I dealt dope.
This was my spot.
Had been waiting for customers.
'You don't exactly ooze respectability' he finished, cheek twitching while he motioned generally.
I was right with him. Appreciated his attentiveness.
Can't be too careful.
Never know who anyone might be.

I SMOKED THE YEAR-OLD CIGARETTE. Kept after the one-act with Damon. Nothing prompted me to.
Lit it from a rough drag of kitchen match to the side of a box which'd been stowed in an above-stove cabinet for a decade, at least.
Well I recall the lights of that office building's parking lot. Chicken-broth colored. The stale scent of the burning tobacco redoubled throughout sour fog by the midnight humidity.
Didn't inhale down to my lungs. Smoke pooled over my tongue. Underneath. Lulled against cheeks. When I'd opened my mouth it poured out. Thick white. All at once. As though I'd collected helium saliva then drooled.

All purely aesthetic. Smoking. Addictively aesthetic. Remains so to this day.

There is vast joy in a cigarette. Having something beautiful to think behind.

Beyond that, I've never experienced pleasure in the act. Detest the jitters lasting ten minutes after the two-at-a-time I'd commonly chain.

The two-at-a-time I still do.

I'd turned eighteen the smack middle of senior year.

Cigs now an attainable, maintainable component of me.

Props too alluring to go without.

Crumpled pack of unfiltered *Luckies*?

My God, is any object on Earth more attractive?

The coughing *klik-ktsch* of a Zippo flicking open.

Curt shush of thumb over flint mechanism.

*Tsk-poof* of flame going glimmer.

The size, weight of these artifacts in concert, their inherent no-good-for-anyone, earns them a grace only the insipid can with honesty chide.

Yvette became fond of the things.

Nathaniel, when home for break or weekends, got in on the scene. He and I also tried snuff. Quickly abandoned it. A shame, as the compact tins of talcum-fine powder were marvelous.

The habit led me to obtain an official State Identification Card.

Thus purchases could be made from cashiers.

So neat, for awhile. How such transactions were permissible under-the-law yet a threat of consequence hung over the act, all the same.

Yvette was yet shy of appropriate age. Her parents would've ended our interactions had they cottoned how she'd taken up such healthless habit.

I rather adored how the risk seemed worth it to her.

Didn't comprehend it.

Didn't want to ruin its purity for trying to.

It was such adoration which led to my being caught. Apprehended proper for the first time in my life. No childhood A-B-C-one-two-three kind of I-know-what-you-did from sibling, parent, or pal.

Nabbed in the act of theft as an adult.

It started as such a thing would.

Skint one afternoon.

No ciggies on hand with which Yvette and I might wile away time.

What to do?

Smokes were kept behind cashier counters. No direct access.

But Yvette pointed out how in most Drugstores there were aisles where cigarillos dwelt. Exposed for the plucking.

She was right.

Her being so, I couldn't see why we oughtn't procure some.

Stout brown sticks, like arsenic cinnamon. Eight to each tight packet. Some with plastic filters affixed to rear ends. Such teasing little pixies. Toys with cancer and rap sheets.

I should've understood what was coming.

Did.

But only exactly too late.

I was breaking my own rule. The one true rule. That theft needed be undertaken for its own sake, only. A motive must be singular. Plural desires made matters dangerous. Suborned disaster. Stealing was a discipline which needed be unshared. Self-contained. Immaculately selfish.

The cigarillos could've been stolen had stealing them been my own idle idea. Or even if another thief had floated the notion. Nathaniel, say. Our shared identity making whatever we fancied each other's heart.

As it stood, the theft was third-person. Outsider. Its reason not whimsical but direct.

The mechanics of the lift itself were rudimentary.

Cigarillo packet went into hand.

Store roamed while fingers manipulated the shrink-wrapping free.

Wrapping discarded discreetly.

Packet-bottom thumbed open while roaming continued.

Contents slipped out to palm, slipped from palm to pocket.

Husk-package stashed. In this case behind bags of Sausalito cookies.

I'd instructed Yvette to hang off to one side. I wonder, still, if somehow I'd sensed things would go South.

Deciding it'd be best to make a purchase with my measly last dollar, I'd moved to fetch a soda from the rear of the store.

Right then, I knew the jig was up.

Even before my eyes, now, I see him. Spittle thin reflection of store security on the chill glass of the refrigerated display. Oily bulb of the man taking position at the end of the aisle. Sway of giddy impatience.

Even were I to attempt unloading the merchandise I'd be done.

He'd have me to-rights for attempting cover-up, too.

I walked with a *Dr. Pepper* the short plank toward cash registers.

Straight away a hand to my arm.

Would I mind stepping this way?

Yvette was leafing through a gossip magazine up front. As I was escorted toward the cashier area, she was clever in not making eye-contact. But I could tell she'd noted peripherally the subtle *go-go-go* I'd swiveled my head in.

By the time I was emptying out pockets as ordered, she'd ambled off premises.

What followed was fiasco.

These Drugstore boys weren't messing around.

First off, I'd be banished from the store. Forever.

There'd be a fine. Amount to-be-determined.

This on top of restitution for the wasted product.

Understood. This'd all been so stupid of me. I proclaimed how, in a way, I was glad to've been stopped. 'I'm not cut out for this sort of thing.'

But further complications, yet.

The theft was of a restricted-age product.

How old was I?

Eighteen. Even a smoker. Just didn't have dough for a pack.

Patted my pockets for ID to prove it.

Nothing there.

Left in the pants I'd changed out of, that morning. Lumped in my duffle. At Yvette's.

This elevated the situation to a police matter.

No, they weren't kidding.

An officer had already been dispatched.

Poor Yvette. Waiting out front. What torment she must've been suffering.

Having to assume me underage, the police officer asked for my parents' contact numbers.

'Thing is, officer, not only are my folks unlikely to be home, home is an hour's drive. Had been planning to get picked up tonight. Time pre-arranged.'

Listen, he was trying to do me a favor. But look at it his way. No ID. No contact to vouch for me or anyone into whose custody I could be released.

Did I see?

Yes. Unfortunately.

Best he could do?

Fill out a report. Ticket me. Court date.

If I failed to appear, a warrant would be issued.

He was extending me a heckuva lot of trust.

Did I comprehend that?

Appreciate it?

I did, officer.

'Okay. What's your name?'

My bowels groaned. Morphed from walnut tight to gassy gelatin.

I coughed. Then mumbled 'Jasper.'

'Jasper what?'

Cold beat.

'Jasper what?'

That face.

'Turn around.' Sting of cuffs snapped around my wrists. 'Tried to do you a solid, my friend.' Restrained fists panicked in taps against my buttocks. 'That's all done, now.'

Time for downtown.

Get me printed.

Wait it out in a cell until contact was made with anyone who could prove who I was.

This couldn't be.

For Christ's sake, no need Yvette be subjected to the sight of me perp-walked to cruiser in shackles, whisked off wherever.

Poor duck would blame herself. Do something drastic.

Or worse, something *sensible*.

Inform her parents.

Call the school.

'Wait wait wait, listen officer. I go to school near here. They might be open, still. They'll confirm I'm who I am.'

Which school?

Okay, he knew the place. 'Last chance.'

Dialed.

No answer.

'But come on, officer, look at me. Do I seem like a criminal? Honestly? I'll pay the ticket. Do the court date.'

Yeah, he knew I would. But first we'd do this. 'Let's go.'

Bounced on the balls of my feet.

Sudden desperate flash.

'What about this? Week or two ago, I was stopped by another cop. Thought I'd stole my own bike. Peddled dope. I hadn't. I don't.'

And?

'It'd been right down the street. Cop'll remember about me, I promise. Told him my name. Didn't have identification then, either. He'll tell you I'd been on my way to my girlfriend's place.'

'Who's your girlfriend?'

Clammy clamp of panic. Get it together, Jasper. 'Her name's … *Loraine*.'

She lives around here?

'Yes … but she's not home. On a trip. Otherwise I'd be calling her or her parents to vouch. See?'

To my honest surprise, he said he did.

I leaned into this good fortune.

'Officer, I should've thought of it before.'

I could give him their contact info, too.

If I no-show for court, he's covered.

My parents don't pick up, call the school.

School gives the runaround, hit up my girlfriend's parents.

That's three ways to find me. I was cooperating. No resistance.

'I'm really eighteen. Split second I get home, I'm calling the number on this ticket. Will prove who I am. Arrange everything. This trouble's all on me. I don't want anyone else hassled.'

I was uncuffed.

Twenty minutes of tedious paperwork followed.

Banned from all branches of the Drugstore, nation-wide.

Three-hundred dollar fine.

Court date.

Number to call.

'You seem like a good kid' the officer said.

Tilted his head I should toddle off.

Yvette was right in front.

I whispered immediately 'Walk the other way, I'll meet you around'.

Jammed hands down pockets. Neck strained from chin touching chest. My gait garish, marionette. Tick-tock I made the progress across Shopping Plaza.

Eventually saw Yvette waiting by a dumpster.

I approached her. Damp with the sweat of my cretin pride.

Tightened my chest to stave off the laugh waiting to burst.

The one I'd spare her.

The one I'd keep for myself.


RATHER A BUM DEAL. For all intents and purposes, since I still dwelt at home, attended a high-school my mom paid for, the eyes of the law considered me under parental jurisdiction. Don't know was I labeled a juvenile, per se. But regardless, a guardian would have to accompany me to my day in court.

Figuring it best to spring this development on my dad at the absolute last possible second, I timed his briefing for a drive home from Yvette's house, late Friday evening. Saturday morning, eight o'clock sharp, would be the event.

Shot the breeze about whatever *National Public Radio* was blabbing from the car speakers. Asked in advance could maybe I borrow a few bucks to buy a book or two, sometime in the near future.

'By-the-by, I was halfway-arrested some few weeks back. John Law insists a legal custodian has to be in attendance while my sentence is handed down.'

So, if he wasn't too busy could he drive me back up in the morning?

Sit in on proceedings?

I'd no doubt he agreed it was better to bug him with such trifles than to upset my mom. She wouldn't know any better than to be ashamed.

'But you can see where it's all a cockamamie mix up, right dad? It's practically satire, when all is given an honest inspection.'

What had I done?

Well, before we got into that irrelevancy, maybe I'd better give some background. Context is becoming a lost art. He'd always said so.

Thing to understand, first of all, was I'd been reading piles of Russian literature, lately. He knew the stuff? Exactly. Raskolinkov and those guys. Also that shorter book by Tolstoy. Which? *The Forged Coupon*. He'd never read it? Oh, he had to be pulling my leg. I'd nab him up a copy next time I saw one.

So all that Ruskie stuff plus a buncha French existentialism, classic *Valjean versus Javert* hijinks, and some German called Hesse thrown in for good measure had been bubbling in my still-developing brain.

What result?

I'd shunted onto some dubious philosophical side-roads.

I mean, I didn't find them dubious.

This was the Scientific Method at its best.

I'd observed.

Cogitated.

Then set to experiment.

Had wanted to do some subversive things. For the experiences. Raw data. Have lived examples to examine the actual currents and feelings of. In-moment and aftermath.

Otherwise my life was armchair musings on hundred-year-old rhetoricals.

Or worse. Conversations with my peers.

Did he think I was gonna really learn anything from them?

Did he want me to go around believing the teachers at the private Catholic school he didn't really have anything to do with me attending had some kinda monopoly on insight?

Ought I ought rather take a peek at things for myself?

'A lemming is still a lemming even if there isn't a cliff nearby, after all.'

What had I done, though?

'Just stolen from a Drugstore.'

Some cigars. Stumpy little guys. Like *Colombo* smokes.

'He's a television detective, dad. Anyway, it's not like I lopped off a pawnbroker's head, eh?'

Had my dad been committed to some previous engagement the next morning, I had no Plan B. Joking aside, I'd truly never have burdened my mom with such guttersnipe matters. Under penalty of torture.

Push came to shove?

Dad couldn't be my wingman?

Hell with it.

They'd have to issue their warrant. I'd wait for the bailiffs to arrive. Go quietly when knuckles rapped on the door.

To my old man's credit, he was none too impressed by the proceedings. Sat in a corner working out math equations on the notepad he carried around with him, perpetually.

It was all the same to him.

As if we were on a family trip to a Pizzeria.

Apparently he'd also been silently judging the figure-of-authority who had been presiding. Later described the man as 'some mere functionary, thinking about and deciding nothing' who amounted to 'not so much a judge' but rather 'a button with a mouth.'

Such a delight.

My pop had added no comment during the brief hearing.

Had put no questions to anyone, afterward.

Hadn't even asked to inspect the paper given me. The one outlining my actual punishment.

Community Service.

Forty Hours.

Considering my age, my school schedule, the sentence would be divvied into eight-hour slots.

Saturdays. Sundays.

Two-and-a-half weeks, consecutive.

It'd kick off in a fortnight.

The venue was a kind of fleabag halfway house, cold-weather shelter, soup kitchen joint. Building itself rather stately. Architecturally gorgeous. Three-story, free-standing. Peculiar in the midst of a slummy district of downtown. Flanked all around by squashed together row-house apartments. Every other one either abandoned or with signs ranging from *For Lease* to *Vacuum Repair* to *Bonds-Lotto-Notary* tacked to some window.

Doing reconnaissance the weekend before my hard-time began, Nathaniel and I couldn't sort out exactly how the place functioned.

Or when.

People did seem to be inside.

But none ever exited.

The house seemed larger and larger the more we scrutinized it.

But had fallen into notable disrepair.

There was construction fencing up around the building perimeter, barring us from approaching front door. We loitered, but no one ever approached us to either get our story or give us the broom.

Meaty suspense.

Yvette and I sat in the shade across the street from the place several times during the week leading up. Smoking cigarillos of the precise brand I'd been nabbed for trying to burgle. Bought legal. From the exact Drugstore I'd been so recently banned from.

Slight haircut and mild respectability of wearing school uniform made a new man of me, it seemed.

Going to the exact shop had been my insistent decision.

'Because' I'd explained to Yvette while casually stepping through the automatic doors to make the first post-incident purchase 'I am an incorrigible rake.'

In fact, I took the avowed stance such cigarillos would be my new trademark. An aspect of identity Fate had determined, from on high.

But I'd never, ever steal them.

So far as I could decipher the hieroglyphs of the life dealt me, purchasing them legitimately from where I was forbidden to be was the edict.

Yvette wondered what would happen if I didn't show up at the time appointed. Still found the entire affair bogus.

I'd had to pay hundreds of dollars for a six-dollar item, after all.

Had no previous, recorded history of law-breaking.

What was this over-the-top reaction to a first-time offense in aid of?

I didn't argue.

Her vexation and questions were valid.

But, curious though I was what would happen were I to go AWOL, I was quite eager to do the time allotted me.

These circumstances all had the whiff to them of the olden times. The haphazard, head-scratching muddle of crime-and-punishment made the workings of the city itself, its comings-and-goings on all levels, seem insectoid.

Here seemed a society which'd been built from summarized blueprints taken from a dozen different out-of-date textbooks. Each member of the Planning Committee under the impression they'd read the same instructions as their companions had. All of them too fearful of embarrassment to call any other one of them out. A world every part of which felt was the only part screwed in backward.

Steal machine-stamped, mass-produced tobacco products from a cookie-cutter chain-retailer?

Be set right by spending just-shy-of-two-day spread out over a month in an anonymous building of indeterminate purpose cloistered in some random part of an adjacent town.

Yes, please. Sign Jasper up for a world like that.

How disappointing it would've been had it only been the three-hundred buck penalty and the phony-baloney banishment.

No imagination in that.

Proof positive of the artificiality of an existence which couldn't care less for individual nuance.

This business I was to endure, though?

Whatever it was, it simmered with promise. Showcased how the world meant something but admitted it still hadn't figured out what.

This was the manner of punitive measure doled out to the iconoclast philosophers in the days before monotheism had broke big. The state-sanctioned consequences it was quite clear the big-wigs were making up as they went along.

'Lookit, we're not really sure we grok what everyone's mad about. We admit that. But people do seem to be quite upset. At you. So. We can banish you … or you can drink this hemlock? Basically we'll leave the ball in your court, man. Talk to your friends about it, awhile. Let us know, Monday.'

The only way progress progressed was the romance of hemlock.

A draught of the stuff had banishment built right in, after all.

Yeah. I looked forward to it.

Yvette thought that was funny.

Probably also thought I was putting on a brave face.

Or was so fascinatingly cavalier.

I was simply in love.

Caught myself checking my appearance even more than I typically did during the days leading up. Would spend a solid hour at-a-time in front of bathroom mirror with overhead fan going. Practicing introducing myself to whoever would be in charge of me.

During my nocturnal roaming, I'd fancy myself a fugitive.

One who knew the pursuit was hot.

How the net was closing in.

Would lay on park benches, dribbling cigarillo skyward in mouthfuls toward clouds and moon.

Giggling over all the ways I might wind up embarrassing myself.

Thought of the terror of flubbing a note at piano recital.

Of leaving the first day of class in a new school friendless.

ROOFING SHINGLES LOOKED mouthwatering. Delectable. Cinnamon toast done the way only someone else could. A restaurant. A mother. Butter succumbing perfect to toast's sandpaper. Taps of the powdered spice leaving no sign of themselves in the melt. Spoon dappled sugar granules only perceptible to the touch of the tongue.

Caressing the rough tops of the shingles with thumb pad, I felt miniaturized. Living as trick photography. Superimposed into some cinema frames. Something which would win an achievement award.

My chore was to mule packages of these objects from the dense pile in the yard area up three flights of stairs, a ladder, to rooftop.

Excruciating labor.

What sorry excuse for muscle I had blubbered like jelly almost immediately. The mere effort of gripping the thick paper covering a pack sapped my strength.

Humping backward in tugs to get a packet down off the top of the mound to the dead grass, I'd hold my breath and buck. Vision blurring. Veins at attention, gangly tangles up forearms.

I dragged the shingle-sets like bodies to stow. Across lawn to porch stairs. Dizzy with perspiration. Wheezing by the time I shouldered my way through front door into the building interior where it seemed the air coagulated, hadn't moved in a decade.

I knew what an imbecile I looked, attempting to negotiate the packets. Hugging them tight. Feeling them slip dot-by-dot down me until the lower edge of a pack rested in the crease of my ankle. Whereupon I'd lift my toes. Stiffen foot. Lurch. Walking as though pegged-legged.

I also tried balancing them in the bends of my elbows. Semi-floppy trays. Or else lugging them up over shoulders in the fashion of beams I was hiking to *Calvary*.

First restroom break, I took stock of the damage.

The skids down me had left the skin of my chest pocked with rashy abrasion. Pinheads of blood issued from my left nipple.

Never had I been put to less intellectual, more meaningless work.

Oh that it could've gone on forever.

Seemed to.

Sublime.

Each time I'd arrive on the roof, I'd have a good look around. Head pounding. No view to speak of. Just crumby streets taking on a foreign affect. The world feeling truly away from, alien to me.

Wondered could I make off with a shingle.

Would've settled for an old one.

From the mess of those being stripped. Sluffing to a spot of side-alley concrete as though dandruff from the structure's senile scalp.

Thought of asking, even.

But I'd be too embarrassed.

Word got out?

I didn't want to be held in contempt by the men I worked alongside.

They already knew well enough I was different than them.

Short-timer.

Tourist.

Their days of servitude numbered.

Mine, merely lettered.

I'd been surprised to be the only one on work-detail who could be labeled a kid. Everyone else middle-aged, easy. Plain felons. Burly, scum-sucking, unsavory types. Or else simply pathetic in ways I'd never dreamed possible even in poems.

The nicer few told me by which nicknames to address them. I'd immediately forget. Too run-of-the-mill to make an impression.

*Big Guy.*

*Bull.*

*Doc.*

The majority barked commands whenever I happened by. As though they were in charge of this monkey-farm. Signed my paycheck. Postured how I'd better stay on their good sides. Otherwise I'd never work in this town, again.

Delightful.

Though some of the novelty had worn off by the third day of my stint.

Even with the school week as buffer, my body had hardly recovered from the first weekend. Indeed, I wasn't rid of bruises earned on day one by my arrival, second Saturday. Was clumsily colored with them. Oblongs of yellow, orange, moss-green, wine-purple.

This time I'd brought cigarettes along for appointed break times. Had felt such a dweeb when none of my comrades had wanted cigarillos.

There'd been one man who'd, for a moment, been excited by

the sight of them. Chap who'd kept wiping the inside of his nostrils with finger through fabric of the short-sleeve of his damp, dingy t-shirt.

He'd inquired whether the things contained marijuana.

I'd told him I didn't smoke grass.

He'd offered to bring me some if I paid him.

In advance.

Most of the day-workers made faces at my cigarettes, too. Disappointed to find them unfiltered.

Though one shady customer had called me 'the real deal' while cuffing my shoulder in gratitude. As he'd ambled off, bow-legged, with four smokes taken, I got the distinct impression they'd caught him, yes, but he never had given up the location of three of those victims.

By the final day of my sentence, all was melodiously uneventful.

I'd realized no one cared who I was.

Or what.

No need for acceptance.

I was just *them*.

A bliss, deeply satiating, coursed throughout me.

When I was assigned to the basement kitchen to scour pots, I didn't mind the room being twenty degrees warmer than the already sweltering upstairs.

I took it as recognition.

Promotion.

No one observing me. Keeping tabs.

A trust extended. Maybe even an understanding how only I, out of all who'd ever passed through these work-release outings, would be capable of appreciating the beauty of this stale sepulcher.

As hours passed in scrubbing acrid cookware with leaky pads of *Brillo* wire, I glanced around for places I might stow myself.

Could there be method by which to steal a night alone in the cobweb of this heavenly flophouse?

Or might I somehow imprint my essence to the listless air?

Leave poltergeist of body-odor behind?

Haunt myself into the room's murky cavity of pipes and rusted, unworkable spigots?

I'd decided to spend as long as it took with a certain bulbous, cast-iron cauldron. Hauled it from the countertop. Its fall left a dent in the mangy concrete.

Under the toothless, fluorescent green which lit my workspace, I discovered an insect down in the vessel's belly. Thick as a fist. Vicious thing seemed too portly to clamber up the vat's inner curve.

I inched it from side-to-side of the circular base with squirts from a nozzled water bottle. When it got to one extreme, it sluggishly about-faced until I prodded it to the other.

After a few laps, it stopped doing that.

Even if I'd zap it with a direct spritz.

The beast had hunkered down.

I tipped the kettle over, thinking now it'd scuttle out.

Instead it nestled itself in the recesses.

As though closing its eyes. Pretending itself invisible.

With ridiculous effort I flipped the awkward tankard upside-down. Thumped on its rough bottom. Texture of the metal akin to asphalt. Or the scab of an elephant's skinned knee.

I think I spent half-hour just sitting there. Surveying what all remained to possibly clean. Understanding no one would know whether I made one further lick of effort. Could do nothing against me if I didn't.

Expecting the flabby pest to scurry mad-dash when I lifted the cauldron aright, I sprang back. A hollow warble hung in the air while the object got settled. Lingered like a long bout of coughing, muffled by surgical gauze.

Nothing was there on the floor.

Or anywhere.

I shushed my feet all around. Stomped. Patted at myself. Darting glances this way this way that.

The vermin was still clung to the pot bottom.

Unresponsive to further squirts of my water.

Except for a one-time, half-hearted lift of wings seemingly too emaciated to flutter.

I gazed down at that idiot bug a long while.

Dreamt a scenario of kissing my fingertips. Touching them to it.

Didn't, in the end. Mistrustful.

But I wanted to kiss it.

Felt so whole and spectacular.

Serenity, completeness welled in me. From everywhere.

I felt secure. In everything.

Known. By everyone.

Loved.

Loved for everything I was and had ever been.

Loved by every person who I'd ever crossed paths with.

Loved by mother, father, brothers, friends.

Loved by teachers, shop clerks, strangers.

Loved entire. Without question.

Loved as though needed.

Loved as though the sight of me brought a spring to the step of all.

For a moment, I did a dance. Formless. Body acting out as it pleased.

Suddenly got shy.

But kept thinking of myself dancing. Knew how it'd look.

Thought of how dancing must've been for the first person to do it. The thrill of invention they must've experienced. For a moment being the only entity to ever express in such fashion. The best. Realizing how they'd forever have stayed so had they kept hidden this thing they'd discovered. Allowed nothing to be shared with the world.

That foolish dancer had thought what a shame that would be.

A shame to watch the world move on without dancing.

So had danced.

Shown the world.

Watched the world dance on without them.

Better than they had.

Weightless.

Timeless.

Watched the world dance them irrelevant.

But owing them everything.

I determined to clean one pot more. Which afterward I would spit in.

But not a single spec of the crust clinging this pot, inside or out, would come clean.

Which made me smile, of course.

I spit in the pot, regardless.

Looked at the barnacled filth beside my expectorant.

Those stout chunks of grime fancied themselves something so much more than they were. Permanent clouds in the stainless steel sky.

Each fancied itself a dancer.

A dance.

Everlasting.

Making the world something less of a shame.

While my spit loitered there. A thief.

Would vanish without scrubbing.

Gone. Like the shame the world had once been.

The shame the world ought've remained.

www.ingramcontent.com/pod-product-compliance
Lightning Source LLC
LaVergne TN
LVHW030318070526
838199LV00069B/6504